POSTER COLLECTION

OTTO BAUMBERGER

18

Herausgegeben von / Edited by Bettina Richter

Essay von / by Martin Heller

MUSEUM FÜR GESTALTUNG ZÜRICH
PLAKATSAMMLUNG/POSTER COLLECTION

LARS MÜLLER PUBLISHERS

Vom Plakat. – Es handelt sich in der Bewertung der Gegensätze zwischen «sachlichem» und «künstlerischem» Plakat nicht um mehr oder weniger Naturalismen, sondern darum, ob denn wirklich nicht auch eine gewisse innere Wärme ein Plakat oder eine sonstige Werbearbeit durchpulsen dürfe, jene Wärme, jener Gemütswert, welcher eben nur aus einem künstlerischen Wesen des Entwurfgestalters und nie aus rein verstandesmässiger Konzeption, Fläche plus Farbe plus Schrift plus Fernwirkung entsteht. Die Negierung dieses Gemütswertes bedeutet das Ende einer kurzen Epoche des Werbewesens, die man Plakat-Kunst nannte, zugunsten einer Werbewissenschaft.

About the poster: In evaluating differences between “functional” and “artistic” posters, it is not a question of more or less naturalism, but about whether a certain inner warmth pulses through a poster or other work of advertising, that warmth, that sense of soul that can only emerge from the artistic nature of the designer, and not from a mere intellectual concept: plane plus color plus typeface plus distant recognition. Negating this sense of soul means the end of a short epoch in advertising that was called poster art, in favor of a science of advertising.

Otto Baumberger, 1932

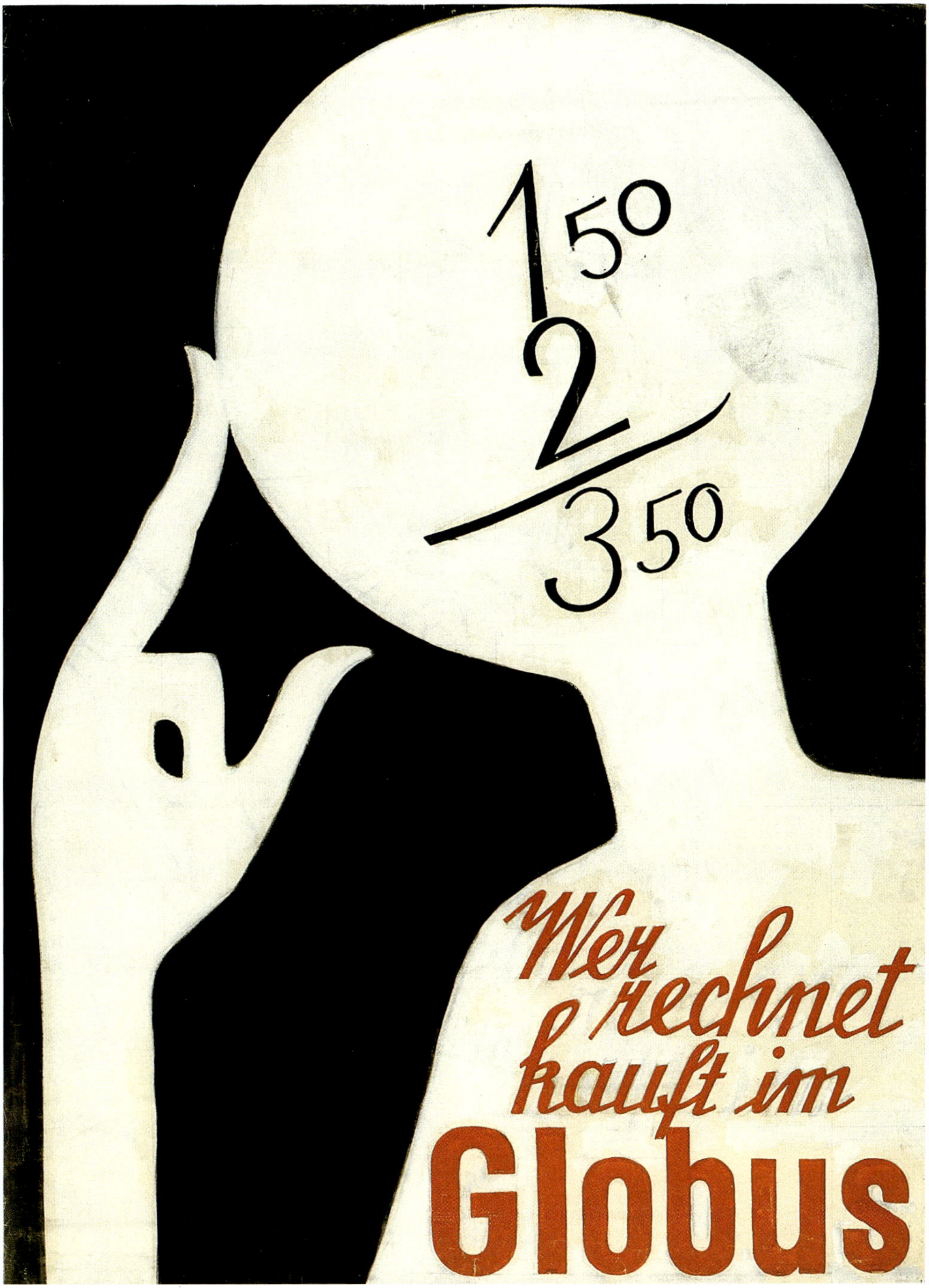

1 **Wer rechnet kauft im Globus**
Anyone who counts buys at Globus
1934

VORWORT

Otto Baumberger – Werber der ersten Stunde: Dieser Titel benennt, was Baumberger als Plakatgestalter auszeichnet. Denn anders als viele seiner Berufskollegen, die sich über einen Individualstil definierten, suchte Baumberger für jeden Werbeauftrag nach der adäquaten Form. Er begriff seine Plakate in erster Linie als Dienstleistung und trug mit dieser Haltung wesentlich zu einer Erneuerung des Mediums im heutigen Verständnis bei. In rund 40 Jahren schuf Baumberger über 200 Plakate für unterschiedlichste Kunden und fand dabei immer wieder zu erstaunlichen gestalterischen Lösungen. Sowohl die fehlende geradlinige Entwicklung als auch Baumbergers Weigerung, sich den ethisch-ästhetischen Idealen zu verschreiben, die den Modernismus im Grafikdesign einleiteten, verblüfften seine Zeitgenossen – und irritieren noch heute den Betrachter. Baumberger entzieht sich dadurch jeder eindeutigen stilistischen Verortung innerhalb der Plakatgeschichte, aber gerade in dieser Vielfalt der Ausdrucksmittel liegt auch seine besondere Modernität.

Baumbergers Ruhm als Plakatgestalter verdankt sich letztlich einem Paradox: Er erhoffte sich stets Anerkennung als freier Künstler, verstand das Plakatschaffen hingegen nur als Broterwerb. Aufgrund dieser klaren Trennung der gestalterischen Disziplinen verfolgte Baumberger nie den Anspruch, seine künstlerische Identität über die angewandte Kunst auszudrücken. Die intensive Auseinandersetzung mit den künstlerischen Avantgarden der Zeit kam seiner Gebrauchsgrafik aber ebenso zugute wie der freien Kunst. Auch Baumbergers fundierte handwerkliche Ausbildung und die lange Tätigkeit als Reproduktionslithograf halfen ihm, unterschiedlichste Stilrichtungen zu adaptieren. In den frühen Plakaten behauptet sich die ornamental-dekorative Vorliebe des Jugendstils neben pathetisch überhöhten Zeichnungen. Schon in den 1920er Jahren wechseln sich malerische, illustrative und formal streng reduzierte Plakate ab. In einigen seiner herausragenden Plakate findet Baumberger zu radikalen, grafischen Lösungen, die Bild und Schrift zum Signet stilisieren. Während einige seiner Arbeiten – die hohe Produktion bringt es zwangsläufig mit sich – mehr als belanglos sind, wurden andere zu Ikonen. Aber nur in der komplexen Zusammenschau, die Zweitrangiges neben Erstklassigem gelten lässt, kann Baumbergers Bedeutung verstanden werden.

Die vorliegende Publikation verweist auf den 1988 anlässlich einer Baumberger-Ausstellung im Museum für Gestaltung Zürich erschienenen Werkkatalog in der damaligen Reihe «Schweizer Plakatgestalter». Sie setzt damit die den Schweizer Klassikern des Plakats gewidmete Auseinandersetzung in der «Poster Collection» fort, verfolgt jedoch nicht den Anspruch eines Werkverzeichnisses von Baumbergers Plakaten. Vielmehr soll aufgezeigt werden, dass dieser die schweizerische Plakatgeschichte in der ersten Hälfte des 20. Jahrhunderts mit ihrer Entwicklung vom malerischen Künstlerplakat zum grafisch geprägten Corporate Design exemplarisch vertritt.

Bettina Richter

FOREWORD

Otto Baumberger: A Founding Father of Advertising—a title that identifies what makes Baumberger stand out as a poster designer: unlike many of his fellow professionals, who defined themselves through an individual style, Baumberger invariably looked for an appropriate form for each advertising commission. He thought of his posters primarily as a service, an approach that made a major contribution to renewing the medium into what we understand it as today. During a forty-year period, Baumberger designed more than two hundred posters for a wide variety of clients, displaying a prodigious capacity for finding astonishing creative solutions. Baumberger's lack of linear development and his refusal to take up the ethical and aesthetic ideals introduced to graphic design by Modernism surprised his colleagues—and still disturb viewers today. While difficult to situate Baumberger within the history of poster art in stylistic terms, it is the diversity in style which gives him a particularly modern quality.

Ultimately, Baumberger owes his fame as a graphic artist to a paradox: he expected to be recognized as a fine artist, and saw creating posters as merely a way of earning a living. As a result of this clear separation of creative disciplines, Baumberger never attempted to express his artistic identity through applied art. But his intensive study of the artistic avant-garde of his day did benefit his commercial graphic work as much as it did his fine art. Baumberger's training as a craftsman and considerable experience with lithographic reproduction gave him the capacity to adapt a broad range of very different styles for his work. In his early posters, the ornamental and decorative style favored by the Art Nouveau could be found alongside illustrations of a lofty sentimentality. Already in the 1920s, illustrative posters alternate with strict minimal forms. In some of his outstanding posters, Baumberger proposes radical graphic solutions that stylize image and typeface into logos. While some of his work is essentially trivial—an inevitable consequence of a high production volume—other posters have become icons. In the final analysis, only by situating those second-rate examples alongside his truly first-class work can we understand Baumberger's importance.

The present publication often refers to the catalogue of work in what was then the Schweizer Plakatgestalter series, which appeared to accompany a Baumberger exhibition in the Museum für Gestaltung Zürich in 1988. While the present exhibit continues the Poster Collection's exploration of classic Swiss poster art and artists, it does not claim to be a catalogue raisonné of Baumberger's posters. It is rather our intention to explore Baumberger's work within the context of Swiss poster history in the first half of the twentieth century, as it developed from a pictorial artist's medium into one of graphic-based corporate design.

Bettina Richter

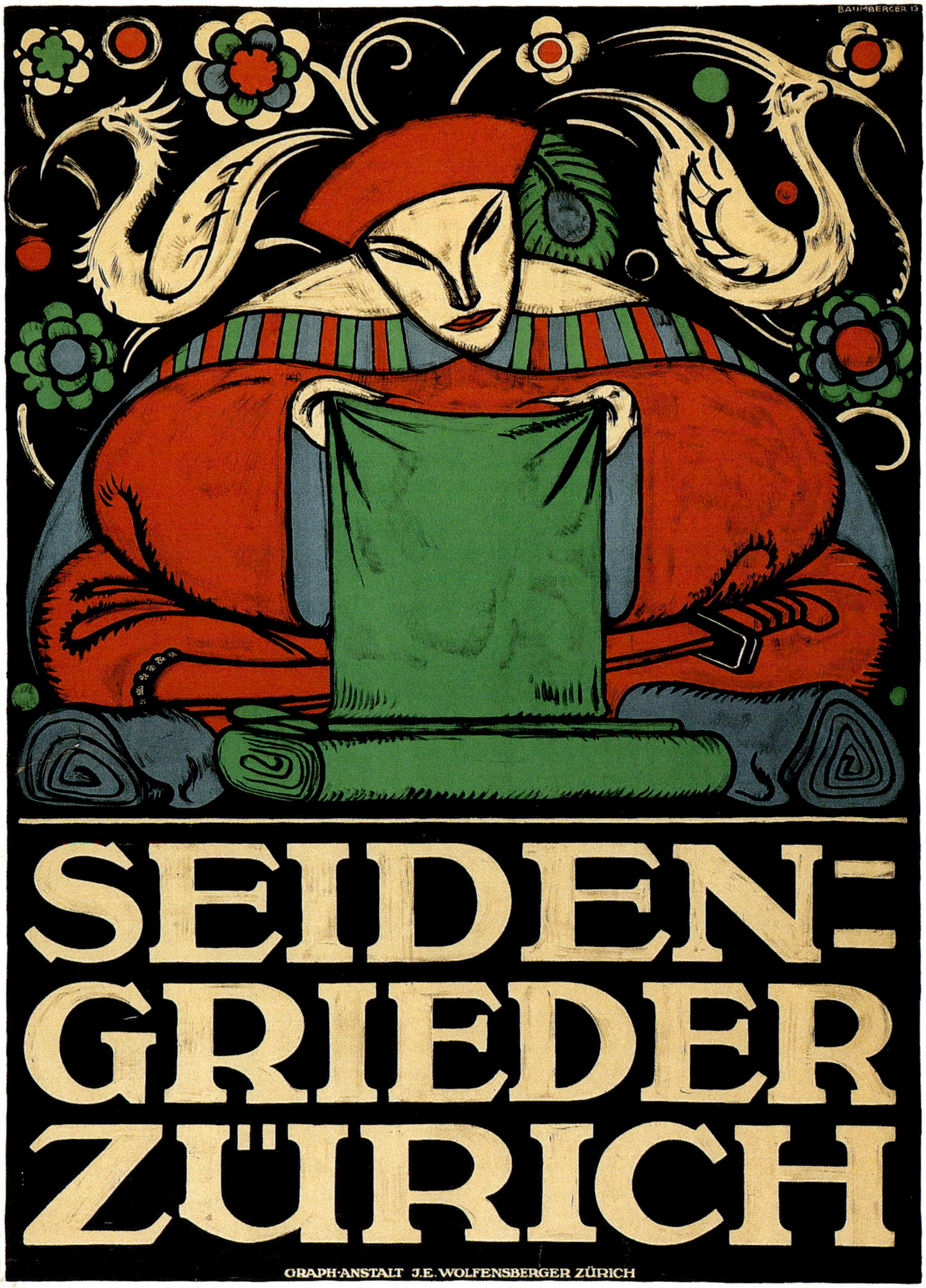

2 **Seiden-Grieder Zürich**
1913

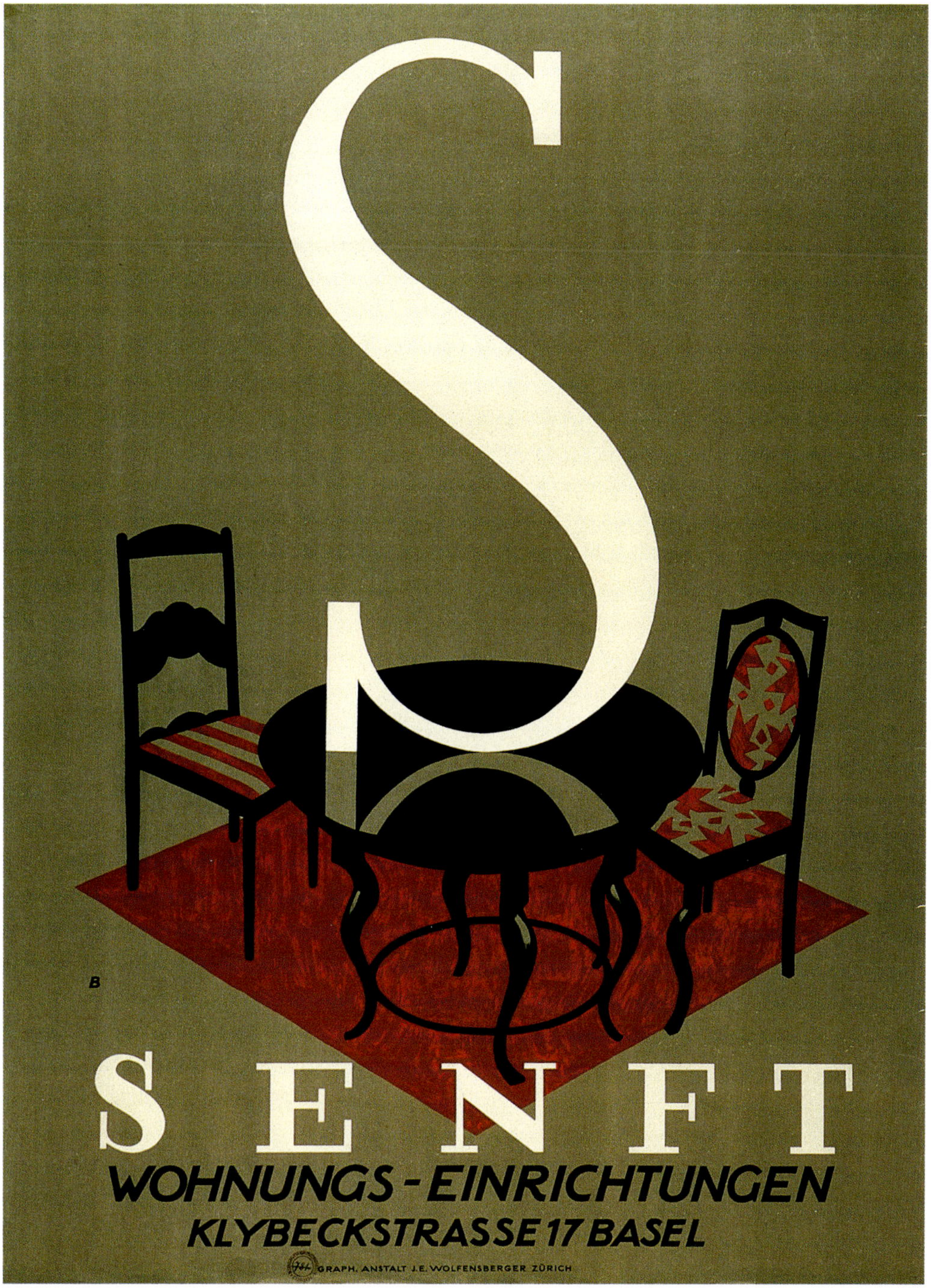

3 **Senft / Basel**
1916

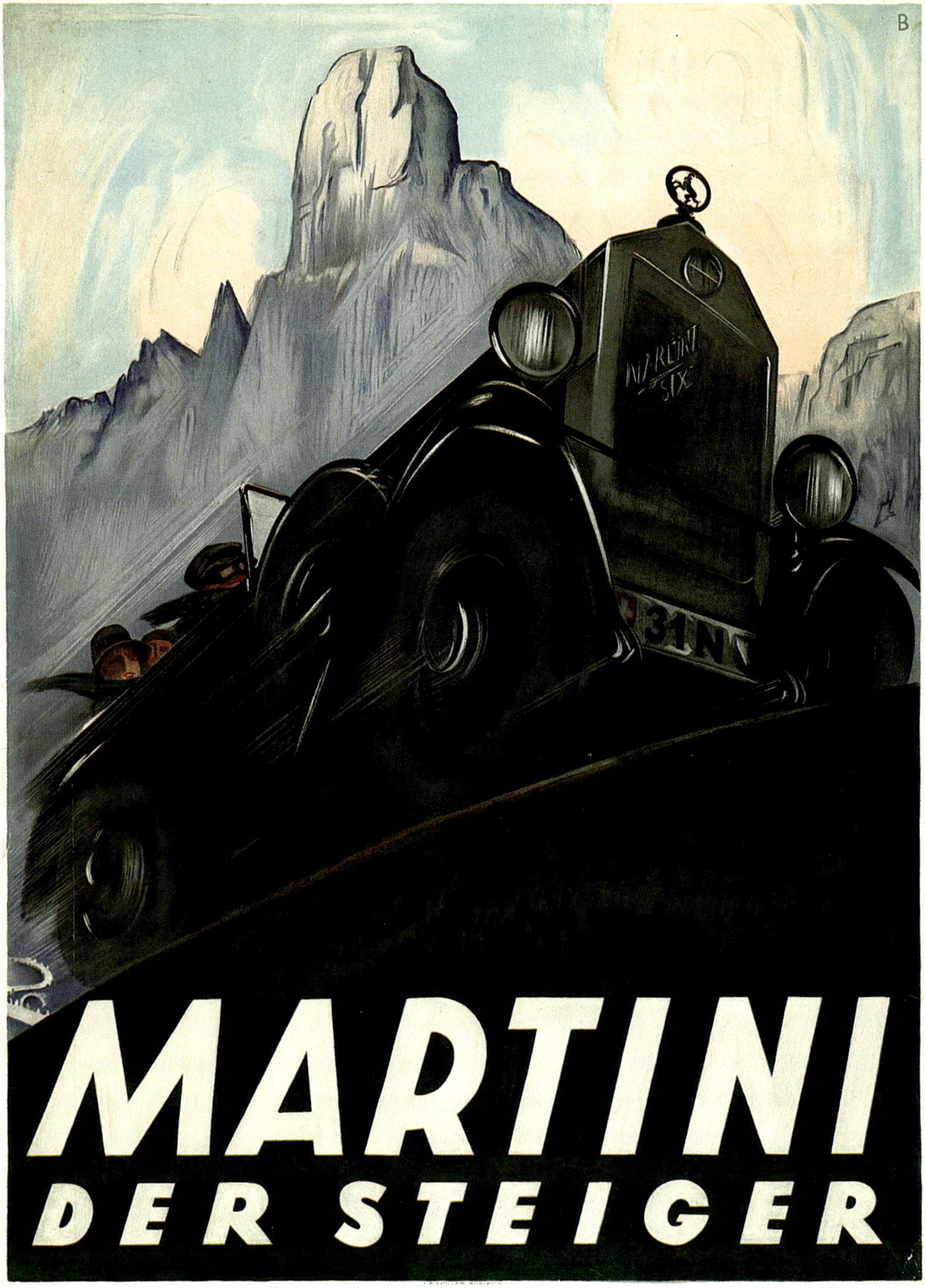

4 **Martini / Der Steiger**
Martini / The climber
1927

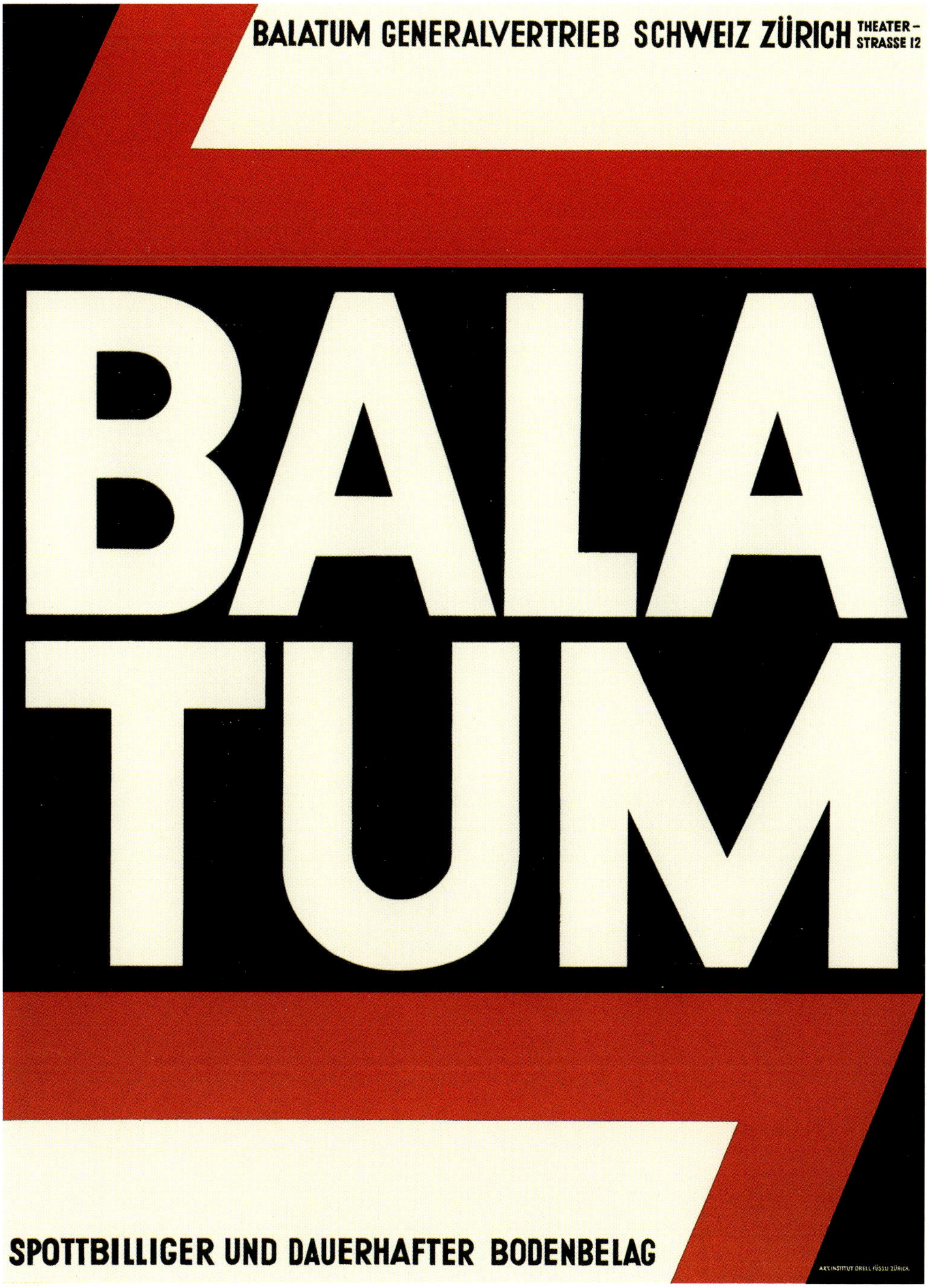

5 **Balatum**
1928

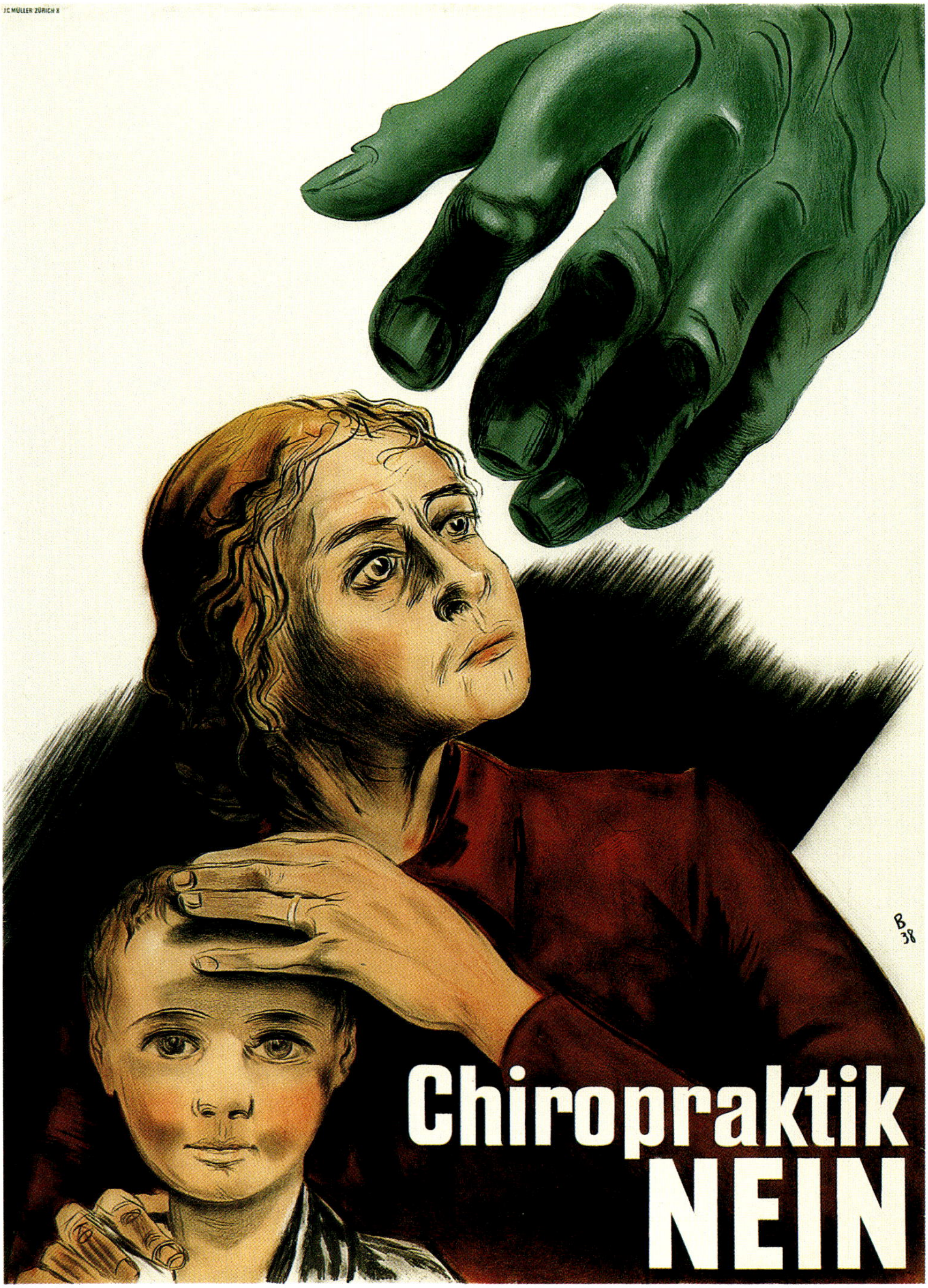

6 **Chiropraktik Nein**
No to chiropractics
1938

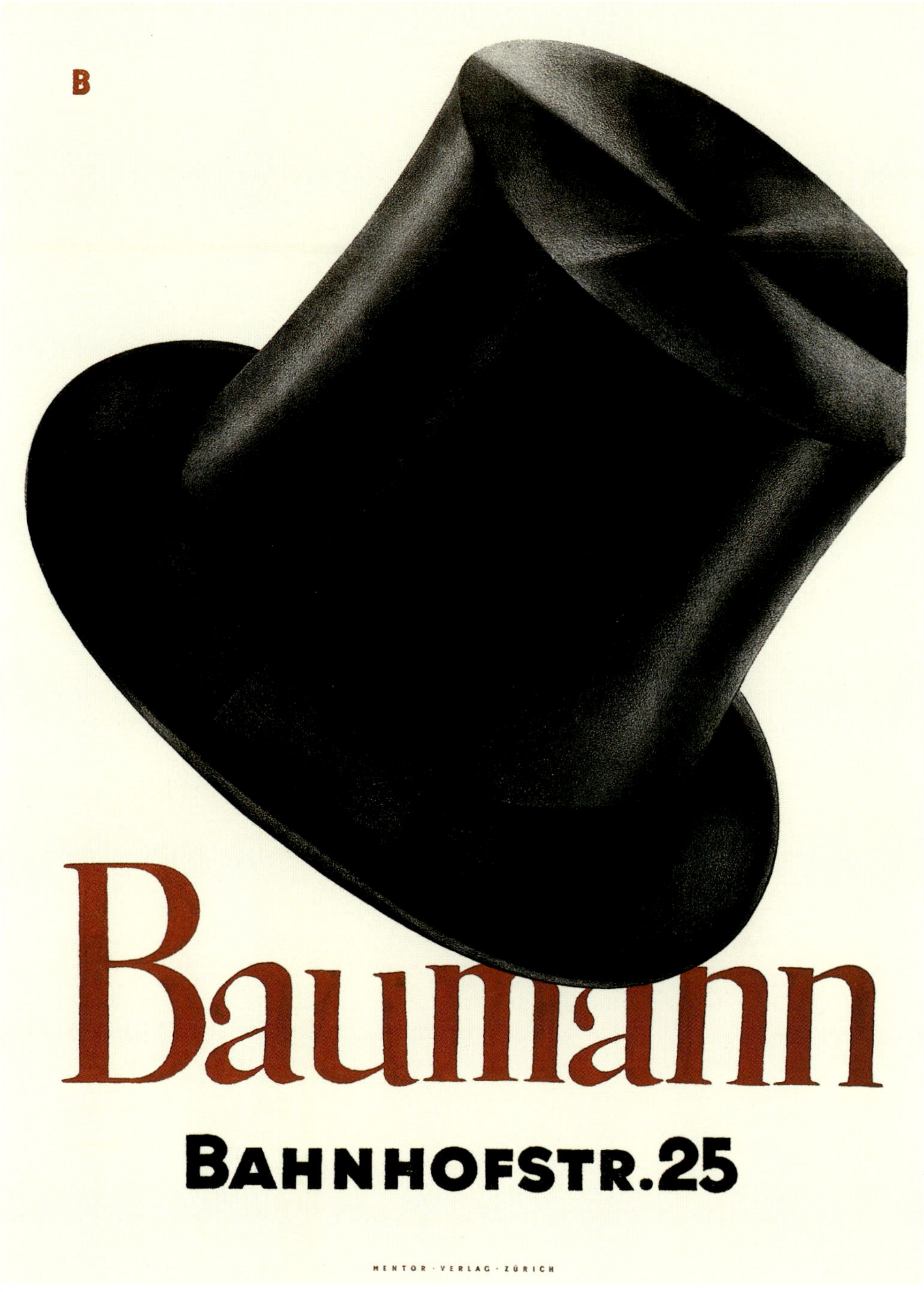

7 **Baumann / Bahnhofstr. 25**
1919

GESCHICHTE IM FLUSS

Martin Heller

Man steige, heisst es, nie zweimal in denselben Fluss. Mag sein. Gewiss ist, dass die Füsse beide Male nass werden.

1988 habe ich am Museum für Gestaltung Zürich eine Ausstellung zu Otto Baumberger erarbeitet. Begleitet wurde sie von einem Katalog mit dem Anspruch, die umfangreiche Produktion dieses Plakatgestalters in einem Werkverzeichnis zu fassen und über unterschiedliche Aufsätze zu kommentieren.[1]

Nun bin ich eingeladen, mir nach zwanzig Jahren dasselbe Werk noch einmal anzusehen. Und es zu lesen und zu deuten als ein Stück Werbe- und Plakatgeschichte, und als Bildwelt.

Wie soll das gehen? Ich vergegenwärtige mir meine einstige Annäherung. Mein Erstaunen darüber, wie viele Bilder und Sprachen der Künstler Baumberger beherrschte – die dramatische Pose ebenso wie die visuelle Posse, Pathos nicht weniger als derbe Karikatur oder biedere Naturseligkeit. Sowie meine Ambivalenz einer zweifellos reichen und zugleich bedürftigen Persönlichkeit gegenüber, deren Zerrissenheit sich oft in schwer erträglicher Larmoyanz Luft machte und doch Höhenflüge ermöglichte.

Otto Baumberger, sagte Bruno Haldner, damals Museumsdirektor in Basel, in einer Vernissagerede sinngemäss, sei der Robert de Niro des Schweizer Plakats: ein unauffälliger Verwandlungskünstler, dessen Identität das professionelle Rollenspiel brauche, um sich überhaupt artikulieren zu können.

LEBEN IM WERK

Die erneute Lektüre von Leben und Werk ist eine seltsame Erfahrung. Der Fluss, der sich mir zeigt, scheint sich nicht verändert zu haben. Unbeirrt zieht er seine Schlaufen durch die Schweizer Kulturlandschaft des frühen 20. Jahrhunderts und behauptet selbst da eine künstlerische Freiheit, wo die Ufer ihm keine Wahl lassen. Baumbergers Virtuosität glitzert noch immer an der Oberfläche, und in den Untiefen dümpelt sein Leiden an jener Konsumwelt, deren Angebote und Bedürfnisse er mit Erfolg bediente.

Offenbar hatte mich meine erste Auseinandersetzung mit diesem Werk nachhaltig geprägt. Baumberger war darin geprüft und für ausreichend schwer befunden worden. Entsprechend fiel das Resultat aus, in Form einer biografisch motivierten Analyse, die weniger ein Heldenepos lieferte als den Nachweis ständigen Ringens um Sinn und um Qualität. Kein Grund also, die damit verbundenen Wertungen in

Frage zu stellen. Noch immer sind «Marque PKZ» 29, «Baumann Bahnhofstr. 25» 7 oder «Fein-Kaller» 52 unschlagbare Meisterwerke emblematischer Markenpräsenz und sparsamer Verführung.

Indessen: Meilensteine markieren den Weg, aber tragen kaum bei zu seiner Erklärung. Noch weniger vermögen sie verständlich zu machen, warum gerade dieser Weg überhaupt gegangen wird. Wahrnehmung braucht Einfühlung. Wer den Zeh ins Wasser hält, sieht zwar nicht besser, darf aber einen Erfahrungsgewinn buchen. Der Fluss wird zur Berührung. Sinnlichkeit ist immer ein Nahverhältnis.

Im Katalog von 1988 stolpere ich, im Bemühen um grössere Nähe, über zwei Textstellen aus Baumbergers Aufzeichnungen. Ich hatte dieses umfangreiche Material schon damals sorgsam erkundet, auf der Suche nach Deutungsangeboten für die in unterschiedlichster Form spürbaren Sehnsüchte des Künstlers. An beide Zitate erinnere ich mich, aber mit einem Mal scheinen sie sich magnetisch anzuziehen.

Ich lese: «Beim Malen an einer Landschaft. Es ist schön, wie ein kleiner lieber Gott im Bild herumzufuhrwerken. Aus einer Winterlandschaft einen Vorfrühling zu machen, die Schneefelder zusammenschnurren zu lassen und in grossen grün-grauen und dunkelbraunen Flecken den nassen schlafenden Rasen und den dampfenden Humus zwischen ihnen hervorzuzaubern.»

Und: «Es lohnt sich kaum, irgendetwas zu bekämpfen – ausser sich selbst.»

Eine gar seltsame Koppelung: Wer so denkt, wirft sich eigenhändig aus dem Paradies. Nimmt seine Schöpferkraft deshalb nicht ernst genug, weil sie zu viel Vergnügen machen könnte, und setzt die Defizite der subjektiven Existenz als einzig gültige Wirklichkeit. Dabei verrät die Sprache vieles: Die Behaglichkeit malender Welterfindung kontrastiert mit der überzogenen Gestik einer moralisierenden Selbstanklage.

SCHWEIZER ERZÄHLUNGEN

Vor zehn Jahren bin ich aus dem Museumsbetrieb ausgeschieden. Manches ist mir danach nebensächlich geworden. Die kunstwissenschaftlichen Feinheiten jener Diskurse etwa, die das «künstlerische» und das «sachliche» Plakat in seiner jeweiligen Verstrickung zu fassen suchen. Oder die Auseinandersetzungen um die zu Baumbergers Zeit neue Theorie und Praxis der Reklame als Teil einer Warenästhetik, die der Moderne ein Alltagsgesicht verlieh. Dies alles kam mir abhanden als fachspezifische Fragestellungen, die von anderen Interessen abgelöst wurden.

Zum Beispiel interessiert mich je länger je mehr, wovon Plakate erzählen. Klar ist, dass sie verkaufen sollen. Aber wovon erzählt ein Plakat über seine kommerzielle Bestimmung hinaus? Von den Bedingungen seiner Herstellung. Das heisst: Von den

Prozessen, die genau diese Bilder haben entstehen lassen, und von einer Kultur ausserhalb künstlerischer Autonomie, die dienen will und dienen muss. Den Produkten natürlich, in erster Linie, aber auch den ProduzentInnen und KonsumentInnen.

Unter solche Bedingungen fällt auch die Herkunft. Otto Baumberger sei, schrieb ich vor zwanzig Jahren, ein Schweizer Grafiker. Das Schweizerische ist in seiner Arbeit mit Händen zu greifen. Kaum je gewinnt sie einen Atem, der über die Landesgrenzen hinweg ziehen möchte. Produkte, Motive, Akteure, ja selbst der behäbige, oft hemdsärmlige Witz dieser Plakate ist schweizerisch, durch und durch.

Dieses Schweizerische trifft mich in einer Erfahrung, über die ich vor zwanzig Jahren noch nicht verfügte. Die Aufgabe, als Künstlerischer Direktor der Expo.02 der Schweizer Landesausstellung Profil und Gehalt zu geben, war eine zweite Sozialisation im Zeichen des Nationalen. Sie hat mir deutlich gemacht, was schweizerische Mentalität an der Schwelle des 21. Jahrhunderts bedeutet. Und ohne den Verästelungen dieser Lernzeit hier im Einzelnen folgen zu wollen, so ist doch interessant, sie hier in Anschlag zu bringen. Um herauszuarbeiten, inwiefern jemand wie Otto Baumberger eine Schweiz verkörperte, die noch immer wirksam ist in dem, was dieses Land heute ausmacht, gleichsam als genetischer Code.

Wobei dieser Code sich in Form von Themensträngen aktualisiert, die Baumbergers Plakatwerk durchziehen und sich darin verschränken. Themen, die nicht den jeweiligen Aufträgen geschuldet sind, sondern dem Boden der Heimat erwachsen – als Leitmotive einer ästhetischen wie sozialen Orientierung unterhalb individueller Ansprüche und künstlerischen Vermögens.

SOLIDITÄT

Solide sind die fröhlich hungrigen, weil in Wirklichkeit satten Bürger im Zürcher Restaurant du Pont 45. Solide kommt der Qualitätsschuh Bally «Farmer» 24 daher. Von solider Brillanz ist das Handwerk Otto Baumbergers, der als gelernter Lithograph wohl die meisten seiner Drucksteine selbst gezeichnet hat. Solid souverän sind auch die Schriften, ohne jede Extravaganz, dann die Kompositionen, die Aneignung von Jugendstil, Expressionismus und Kubismus. Selbst die touristisch überhöhten Landschaften sind derart solide gefügt, als müsse man die Reisenden aus dem In- und Ausland davon überzeugen, dass hier weder Unechtes noch Unrechtes Platz findet 90. Es ist, als hörte man in Otto Baumbergers Plakaten den sicheren Tritt unserer Nation und ihren gleichmässigen Atem. Umgekehrt ist hier niemand unsolide oder gar frivol – das käme schlecht an im Land der Selbstgerechtigkeit, selbst unter den Vorzeichen der Globalisierung.

STADTLAND

Die Rede vom Stadtland Schweiz ist Teil eines aktuellen Diskurses. Sie bringt ein Territorium auf den Begriff, das mental und politisch noch immer den tradierten Gegensatz zwischen Stadt und Land vor sich her trägt, in Wirklichkeit aber längst durch ein komplexes Gefüge von mehrheitlich Agglomerationen samt urbanen, teils metropolitanen Zonen bestimmt ist. Baumbergers Plakate liefern dazu einen unerwarteten Kommentar aus fast schon anachronistischer Frühzeit. Ländliche und städtische Schweiz verschmelzen bei ihm zu einer weitgehend kohärenten Bildlichkeit 93. Zwar sind die Konsumwelten sehr wohl auf unterschiedliche Publikumssegmente ausgerichtet. Aber zum einen ist die Skala dazwischen schleifend, und, zum andern gibt es im Panorama von Baumbergers Plakatschweiz eine Grundtonalität der gebremsten Idylle, der städtische Eleganz ebenso zugänglich ist wie ländliche Unangreifbarkeit.

NEUTRALITÄT

Natürlich geht es da nicht um die politische Doktrin der Neutralität. Auffallend ist vielmehr eine bestimmte Imprägnierung von Baumbergers Bildfindungen durch die Tatsache, dass es kaum je ernst gilt in der Schweiz. Auch da nicht, wo der politische Kampf aufzuflackern scheint und Baumberger problemlos nicht allein die Stile, sondern auch die Seiten wechselt 20, 21. Oder wo Militärflugzeuge lediglich für das Publikum fliegen 66 und Maskenbälle anscheinend keine opulente Festivitäten waren, sondern blosse Maskeraden 17. Und wo sich das Gefühl einstellen mag, Baumbergers oft vergeistigte, dann wieder schemenhafte oder, buchstäblich, plakative Menschen würden sich aus dem Weltgeschehen heraushalten und seien unfähig, wirklich Hand anzulegen. Neutralität ist spürbar als gesellschaftliche Tugend sowie als latente Bereitschaft zum vorauseilenden Rückzug aus allem, was irgendwann unkontrollierbar werden könnte.

FREMDHEIT

Was erträgt die Schweiz an Fremdem? Fremd sind bei Otto Baumberger die Steinfels-Bilder – illustrative Weltblicke zum Einkleben in Sammelalben 63, 80. Oder der Orient, der sich über Produkte wie Zigaretten, Seifen, Füllfedern, Textilien oder Teppiche andient 13. Oder die Tiere des Zürcher Zoos, bewährte vierbeinige oder gefiederte Freunde aus aller Welt 69. Oder es sind die Verheissungen der Kinematografen, in denen die Leinwand zur Projektionsfläche wird für alles, was sich jenseits der Schweizer Grenze abspielt 64. Natürlich ist diese säuberliche Trennung zwischen Eigenem und Fremdem in der Schweiz von heute obsolet. Aber sie bestimmt noch immer einen Teil durchaus populärer Selbstwahrnehmung, die als politisches Potenzial etwelche Begehrlichkeiten weckt. Fremdes ist willkommen, solange es farbig ist, geheimnisvoll, anrührend, distanziert: exotisch eben. Entfällt diese Exotik, so entfällt jede Schlüssigkeit der Bilder. Es sei denn als Diffamierung des Fremden im Eigenen – jener monströsen Frauen etwa, die Gleichberechtigung fordern 28.

ANGST

Es ist kein Strahlen in Baumbergers Plakaten, kein Grundrauschen der Heiterkeit. Stattdessen regiert die Angst. Selten nur erhält sie ein Gesicht wie das des Stadtpolizisten, der über Telefon 17 gerufen werden kann 47. Oder vielleicht besser doch nicht? Denn Hilfe und Strafe liegen nahe beieinander. Viel öfters ist die Angst einfach da, sitzt in den Augen, tarnt sich als Verzagtheit oder als Schatten, bewahrt das Schweizerkreuz vor unbedachtem Zugriff 79 oder traut sich nicht, das Vergnügen des Machens oder des Sehens auszuleben. Und wir erinnern uns: Kein Kampf, denn er lohnt sich kaum – es sei denn gegen einen selbst. Diese Urangst und diese Selbstzweifel sind es, welche die politische Rechte über die letzten Jahre hinweg in aller Unsäglichkeit, aber unter Berufung auf die Mehrheit des Volkes oder zumindest auf ihre eigene Klientel bewirtschaftet hat. Als Schweizer Rohstoff, der sich offenbar problemlos erneuert, seit Jahrzehnten.

GRENZEN DER DEUTBARKEIT

Die Füsse sind nass geworden. Natürlich ist Otto Baumbergers Welt nicht die meine. Aber ich habe sie in Beziehung gesetzt zu einem Teil dessen, was ich im täglichen Sehen und Handeln erfahre. Das Lebenswerk dieses überbegabten Künstlers, der künstlerisch Grosses erfinden wollte und stattdessen illustrierte, was bereits da war, im Plakat ebenso wie in den freien zeichnerischen Arbeiten und Zyklen, ist mir auf andere Weise näher gekommen als in meiner ersten Begegnung.

Es gibt aus dem Jahre 1943 eine Folge von Plakaten für das Rote Kreuz, in denen Baumberger das Elend des Krieges zur Darstellung bringt. In Einzelfiguren, hohlwangig, verschattet, stereotype Kriegsopfer, stellvertretend für Tausende anderer. Das einzige Motiv, das sich solcher Schematik zu entziehen vermag, ist ein Selbstporträt 71. Baumberger hat sich, 54 Jahre alt, als Internierter gezeichnet, müde, schwer, den Kopf auf die Hand gestützt, den Blick zum Boden gewandt. Als existierte kein Aussen mehr, an dem die Augen Gefallen finden könnten, kein Raum, kein Ziel.

Es macht den Anschein, als hätte dieser Otto Baumberger den Kampf gegen sich selbst verloren, oder aufgegeben, ihn vielleicht gar nie wirklich und konsequent geführt. Nur: Darf ein solches Bild, darf ein Zitat eine Deutung nahelegen, die all das einschliesst und wertet, was sich in den über 200 Plakaten von Baumbergers Hand manifestiert?

Denn anders herum ist ja jede Spekulation über die Selbstgewissheit wie auch über die Brüche und Verletzlichkeiten bei Baumberger nur möglich, weil sich in seiner gestalterischen Produktion eine Existenz angreifbar macht. In ihrer Vorliebe für bestimmte Formeln und Lösungen, in ihrer künstlerischen Suche, im oft dezidierten, dann aber wieder auch unbewussten Reagieren auf Freiheiten und Zwänge der jeweiligen Zeit, der Auftraggeber, der eigenen Ambition.

JENSEITS DER WÜNSCHE

An diesem Punkt erst wird mir ein nochmals anderer Wechsel der Perspektive klar, der in der doppelten Lektüre liegt. Vor zwanzig Jahren war mir der Begriff des Lebenswerks eine mehr oder weniger abstrakte Grösse. Er hatte zu tun mit dem Blickwinkel, der sich statt Einzelwerken eine stattliche Menge von Daten und Materialien vornahm. Mehr Stoff stellte ein höheres Mass an Möglichkeiten und Spielformen des Zugriffs in Aussicht. Dass sich damit aber zugleich eine andere Qualität von Wahrnehmungen eröffnet, blieb mir noch verborgen.

Heute bin ich 56 Jahre alt, zwei Jahre älter als der – möglicherweise – in Konsequenz seiner persönlichen Entwicklung internierte, das heisst in seiner Innenwelt eingeschlossene Baumberger. Das bedeutet noch keine Gemeinsamkeit. Aber das vergleichbare Alter macht sensibel für eine doch existenziellere Dimension – für Fragen nach dem vitalen Gewicht eines Werks, nach dem Sinn und der Gültigkeit von Bilanzierungen. Sowie nach der Rechtfertigung eines Vertrauens in jenen Gang der Welt, der weit mehr ist als eine Bildergeschichte.

Kann Wasser, kann ein Fluss altern? Oder sind es doch bloss die Füsse?

In der Nachkriegszeit hat Baumberger kaum mehr Plakate gestaltet. Seine Zeit war, wie das ebenso simpel wie auch brutal heisst, vorbei. Auch verschaffte ihm eine Lehrtätigkeit an der ETH wohl grössere ökonomische Freiheit. Neben breit angelegten Illustrationszyklen zur Bibel und zu bedeutenden Werken der Weltliteratur entstanden bis an sein Lebensende im Jahre 1961 ungefähr 200 abstrakte Kompositionen, die – so nachzulesen bei Wikipedia – weitgehend unbekannt geblieben sind.

1 *Otto Baumberger 1889–1961*, Reihe Schweizer Plakatgestalter 4, hrsg. von Martin Heller, Ausstellungskatalog Museum für Gestaltung Zürich, Zürich 1988.

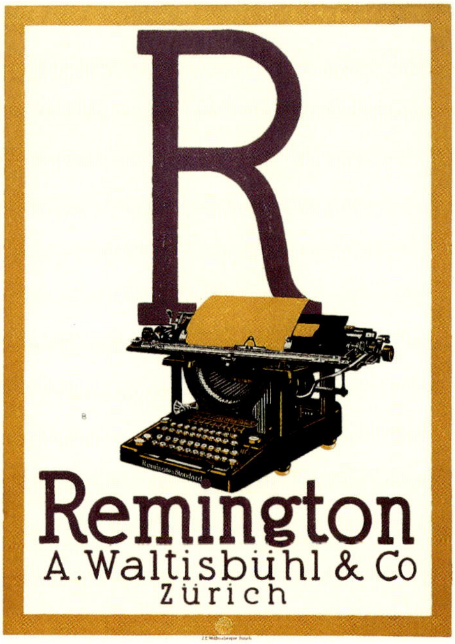

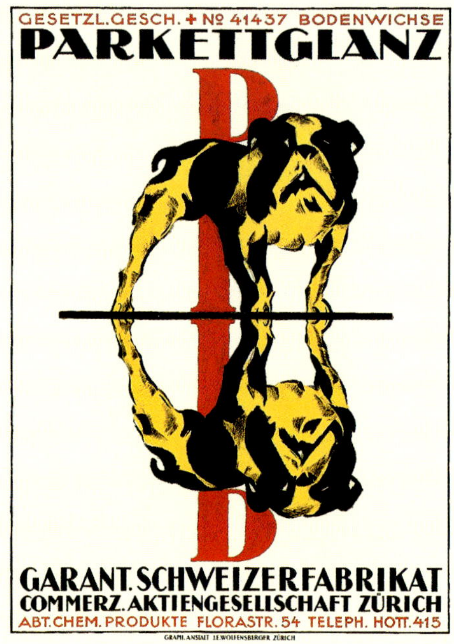

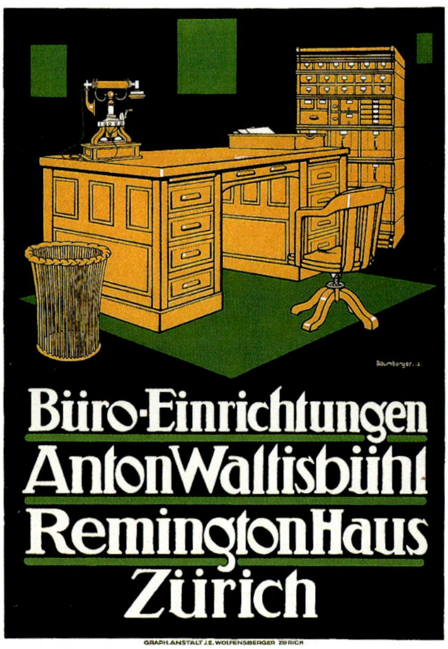

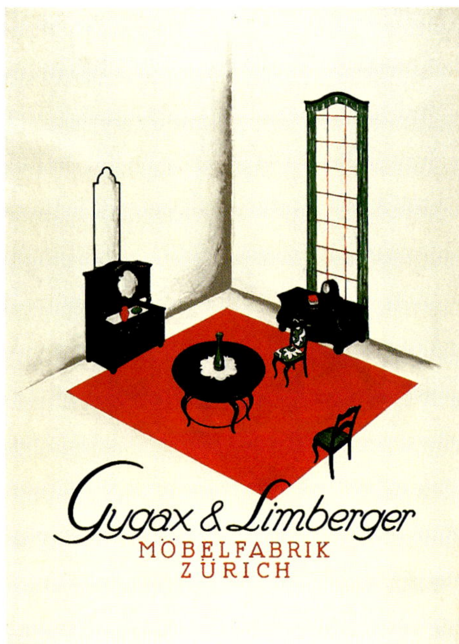

8 **Remington / A. Waltisbühl & Co Zürich**
ca. 1918

9 **Büro-Einrichtungen Anton Waltisbühl**
Anton Waltisbühl office furnishings
1912

10 **Bodenwichse Parkettglanz**
Parkettglanz floor wax
ca. 1921

11 **Gygax & Limberger / Möbelfabrik Zürich**
Zurich furniture factory
1911

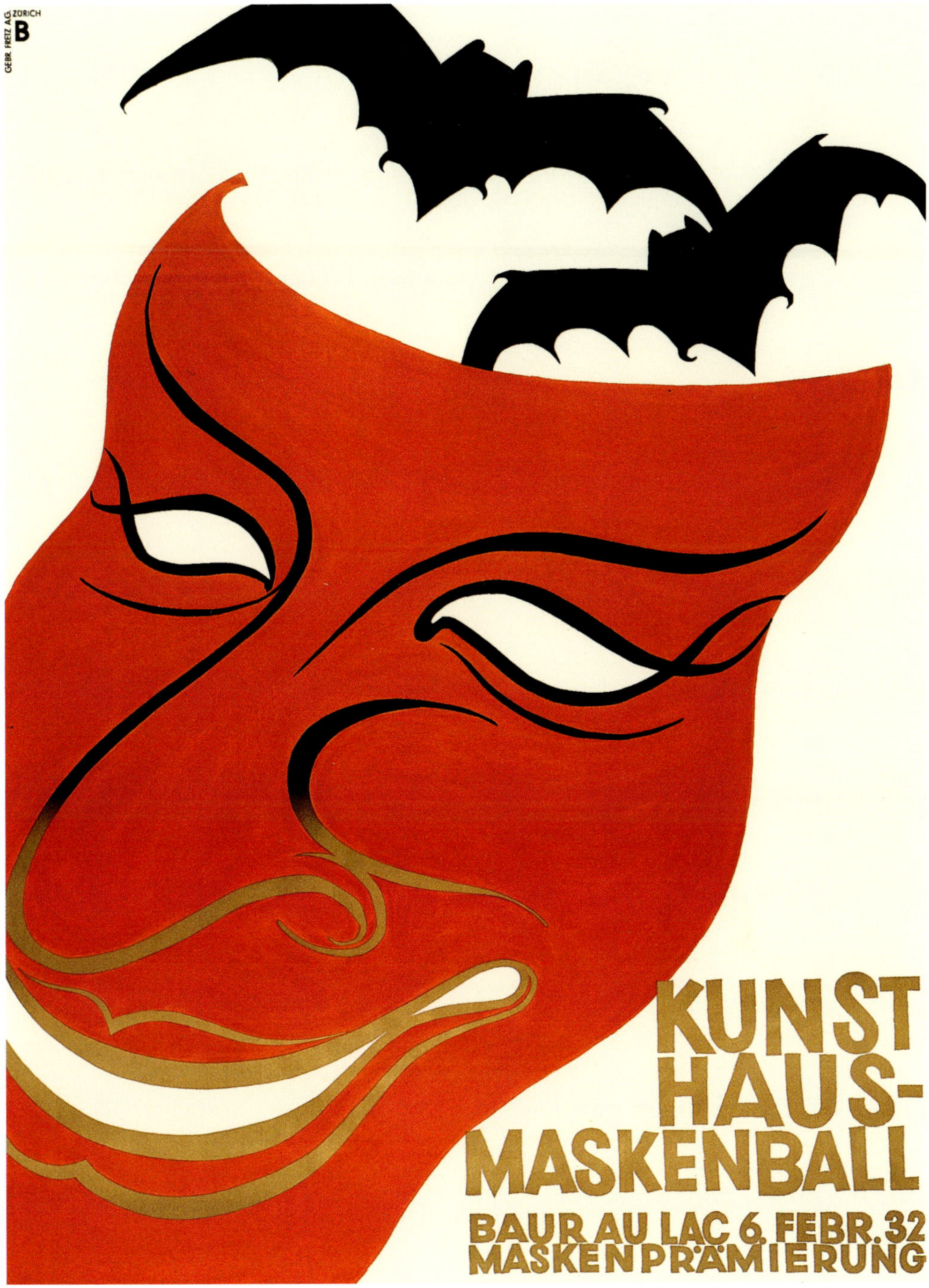

12 **Kunsthaus-Maskenball**
Kunsthaus Masked ball
1932

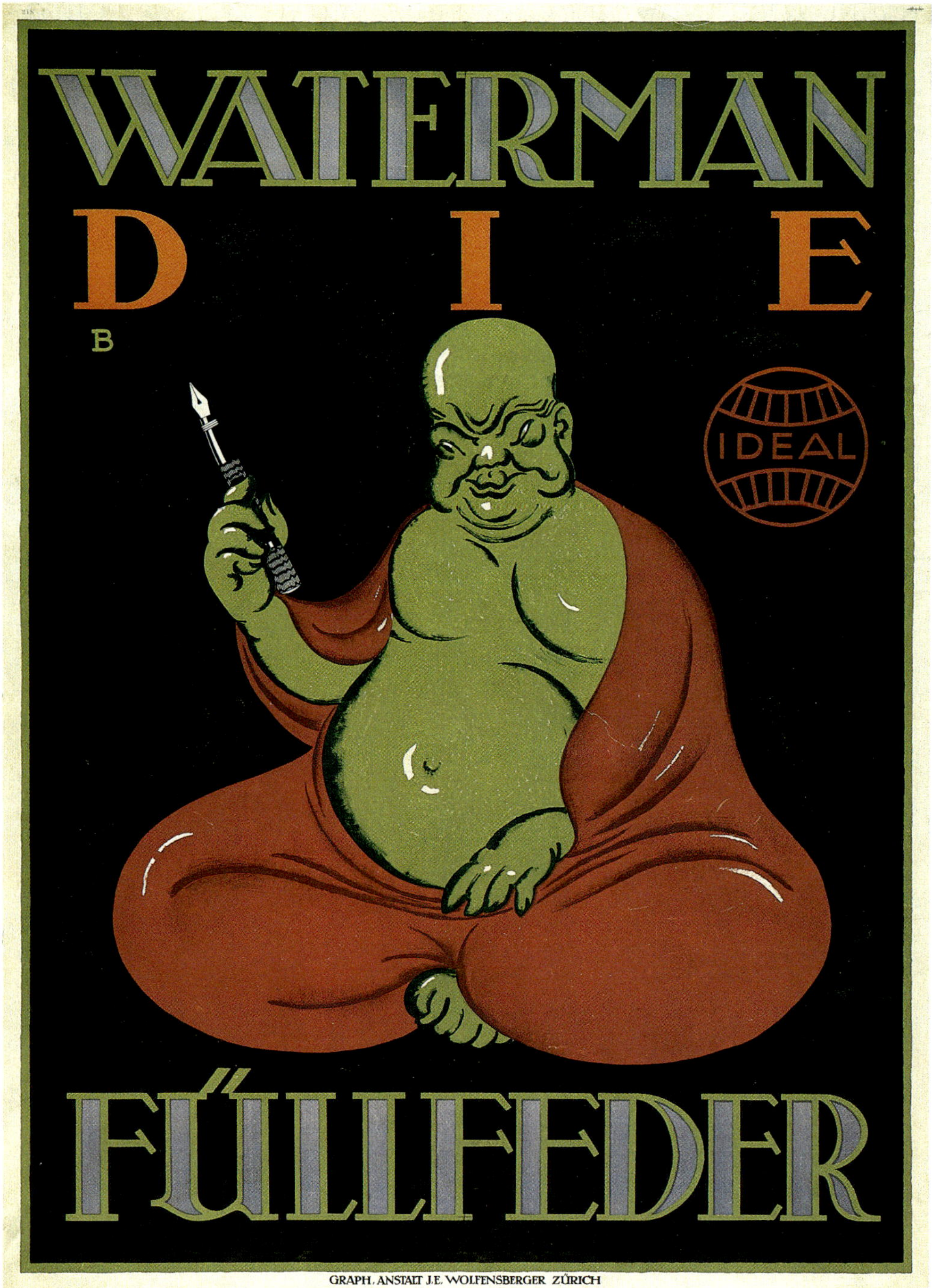

13 **Waterman / Die Füllfeder**
Waterman / The fountain pen
1915

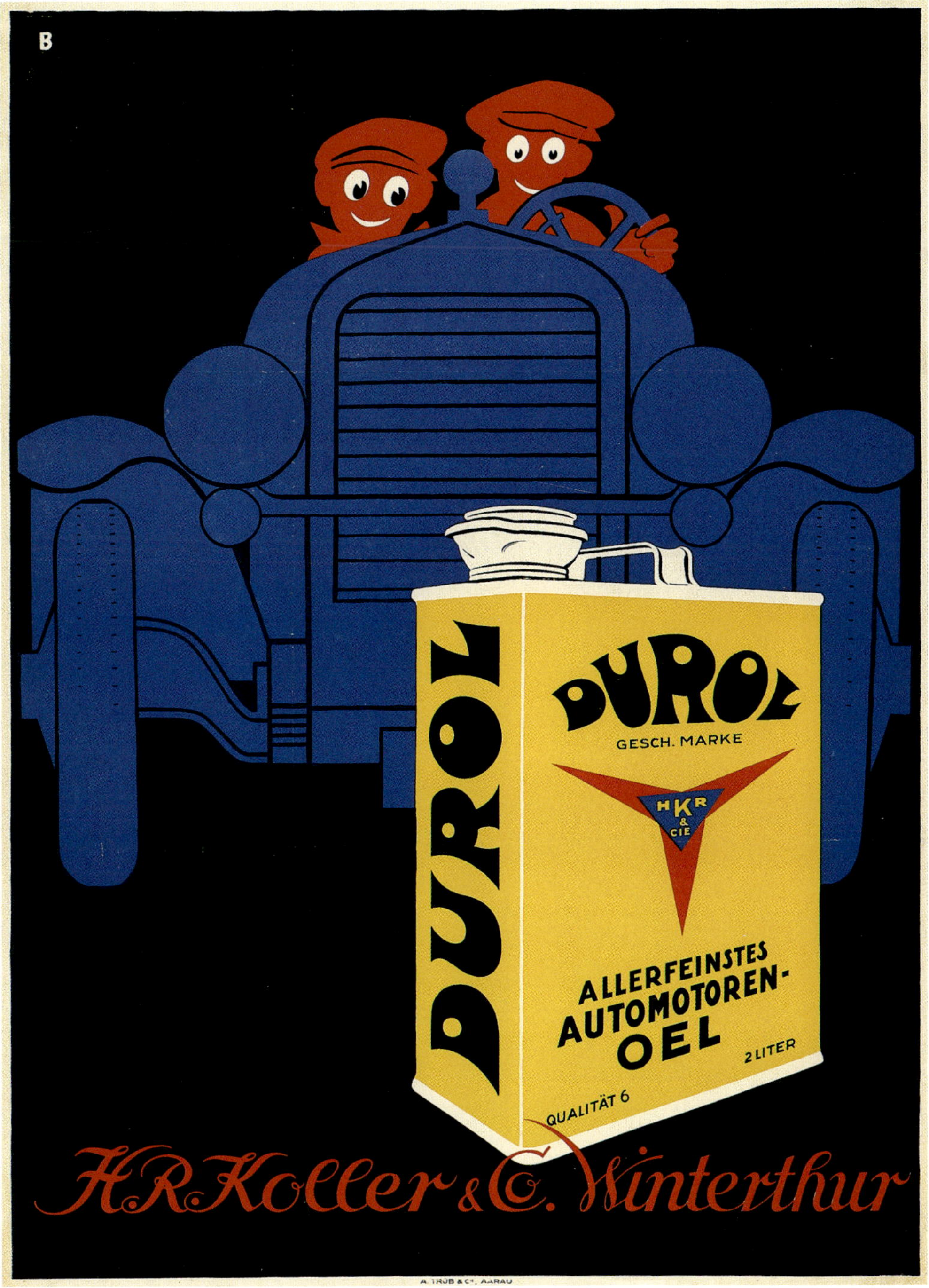

14 **Durol / Allerfeinstes Automotoren-Oel**
Durol / The very finest motor oil
ca. 1923

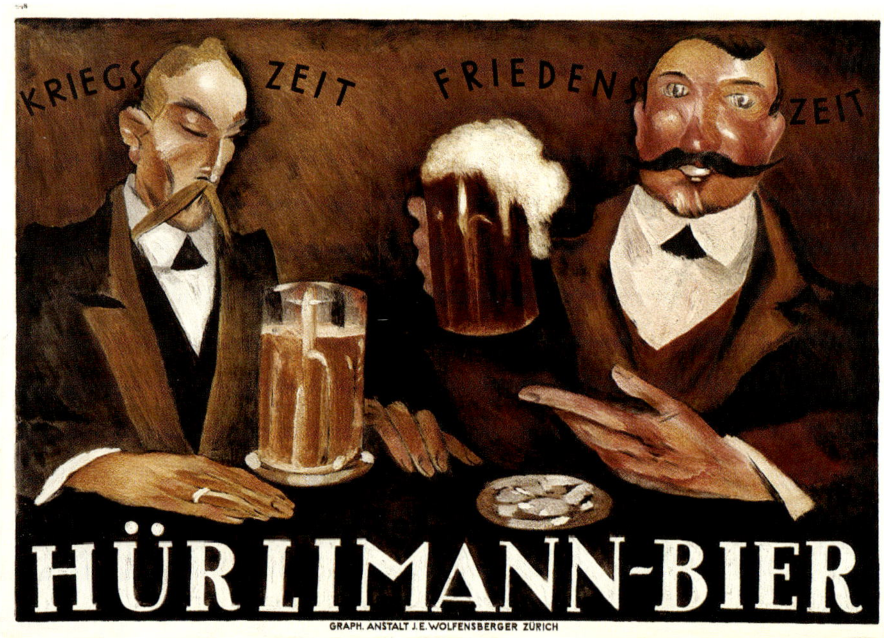

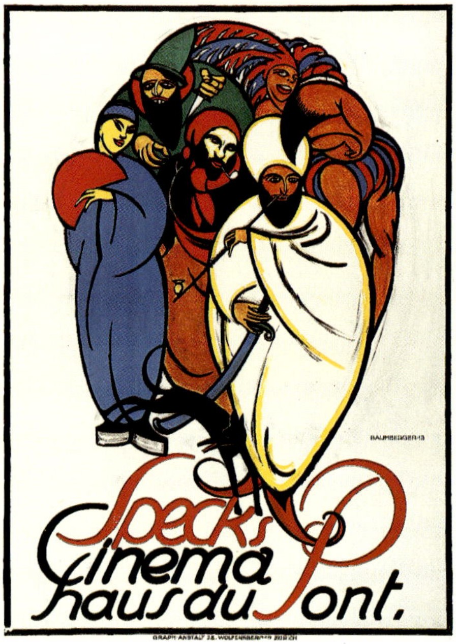

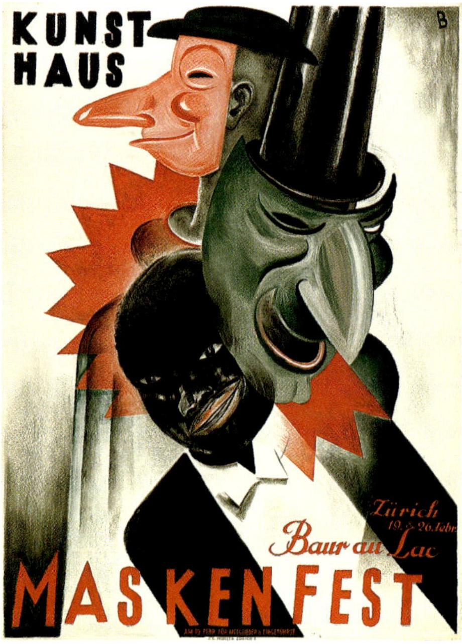

15 **Hürlimann-Bier / Kriegszeit / Friedenszeit**
Hürlimann Beer / Wartime / Peacetime
ca. 1920

16 **Speck's Cinema / Haus du Pont.**
1913

17 **Kunsthaus / Maskenfest**
Kunsthaus / Masquerade party
1926

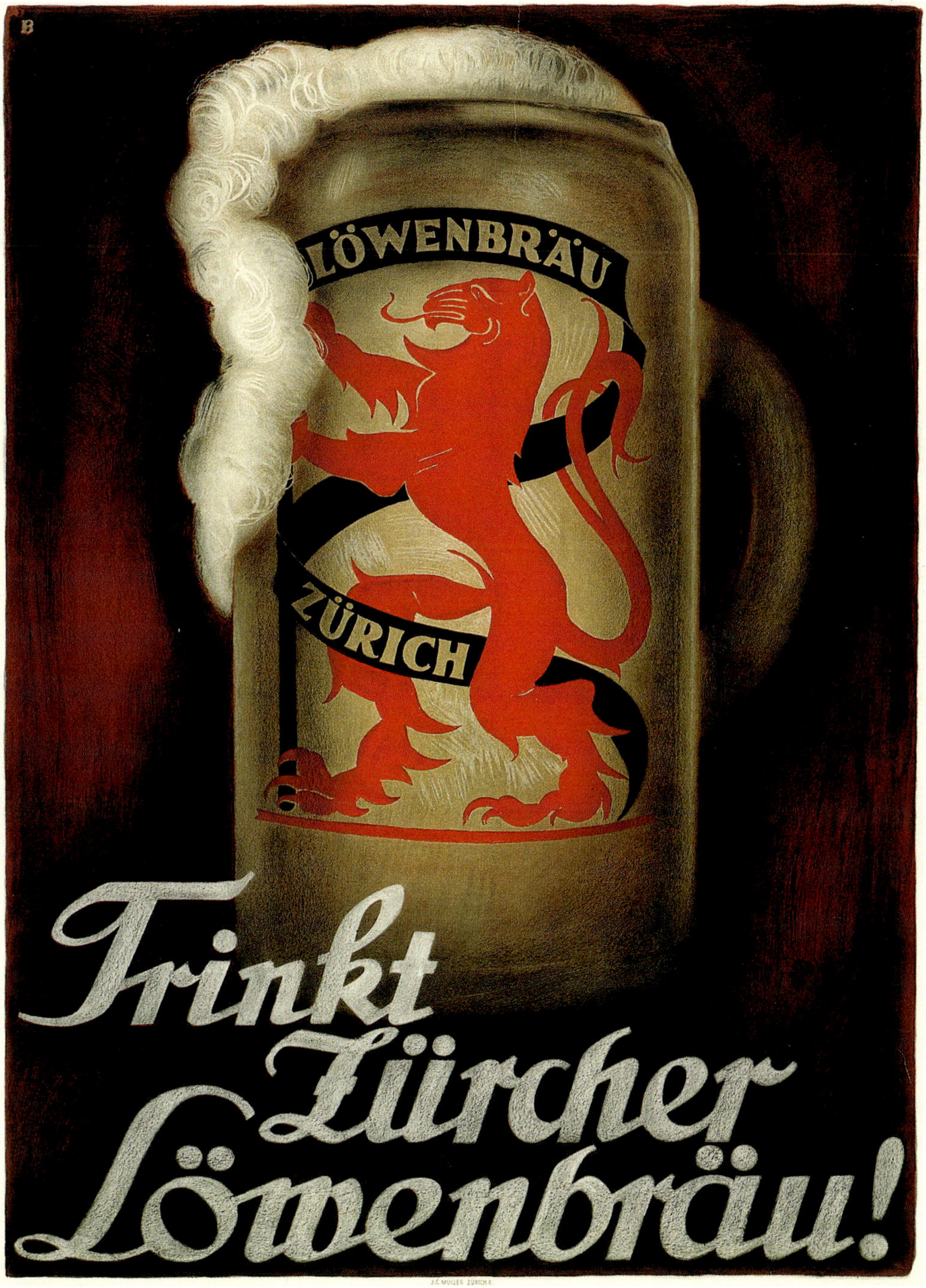

18 **Trinkt Zürcher Löwenbräu!**
Drink Zurich Löwenbräu!
1927

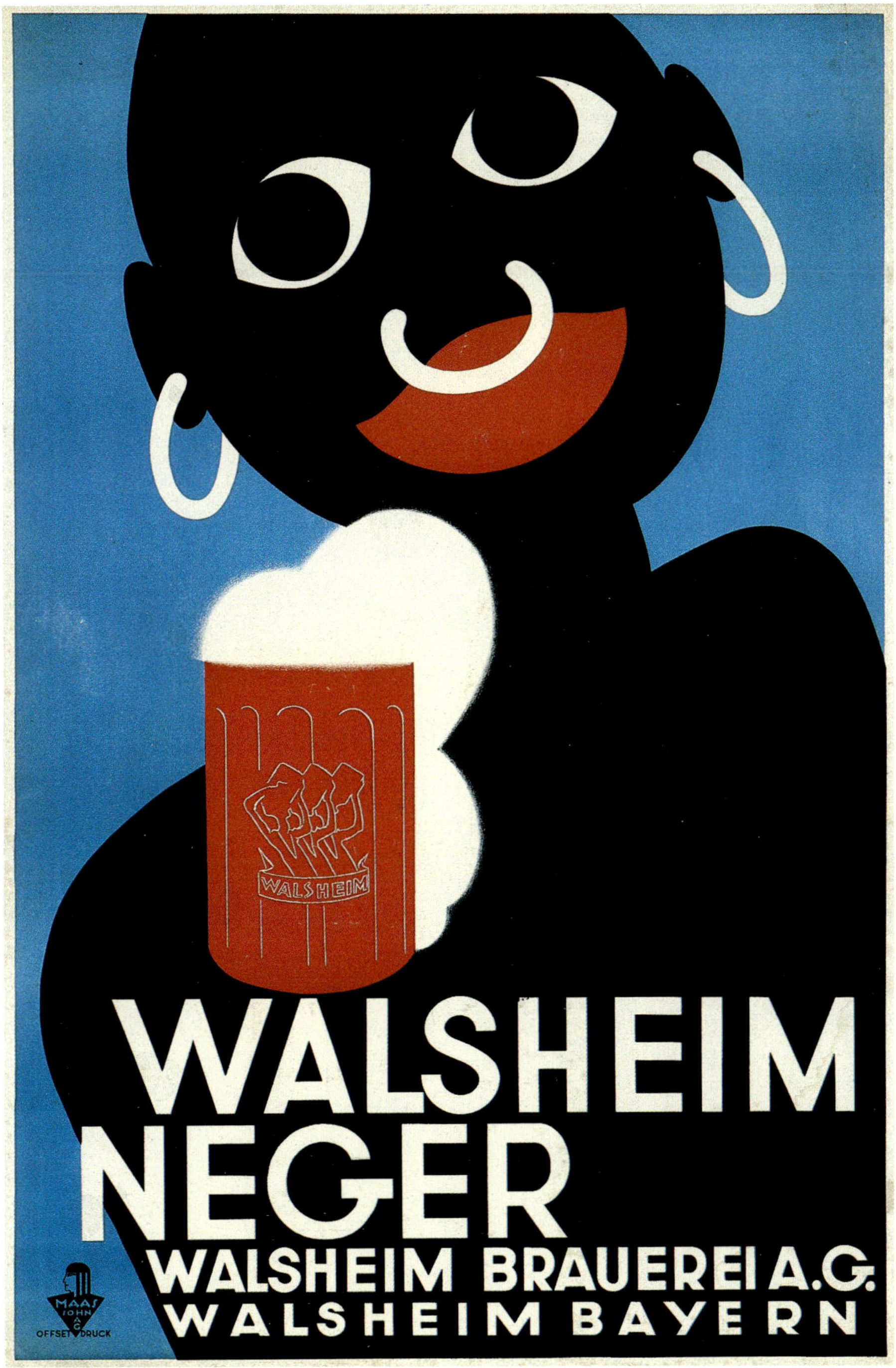

19 **Walsheim Neger / Walsheim Brauerei A.G.**
Walsheim dark beer
1929

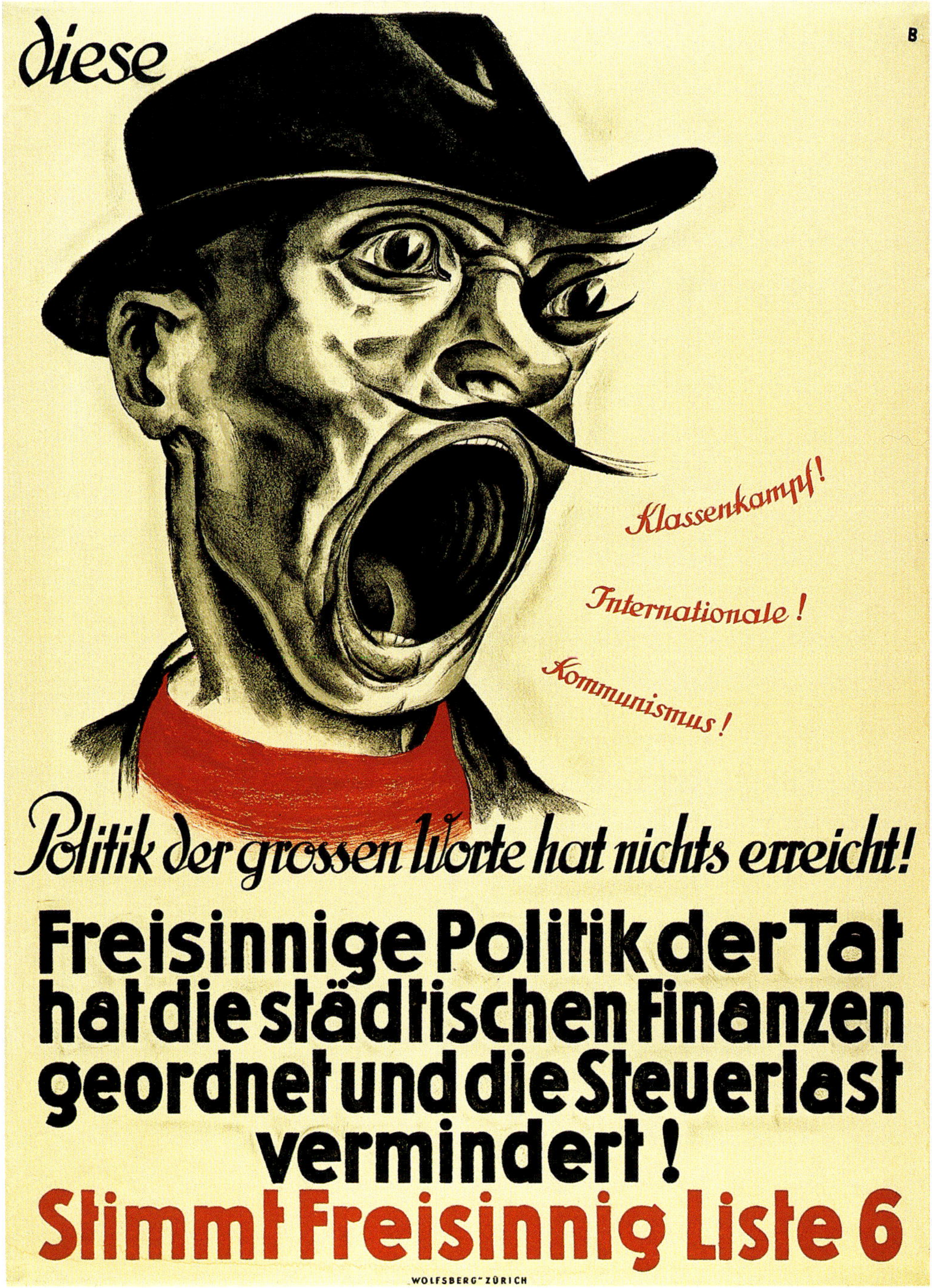

20 **Stimmt Freisinnig Liste 6**
Vote Freisinnig List 6
ca. 1925

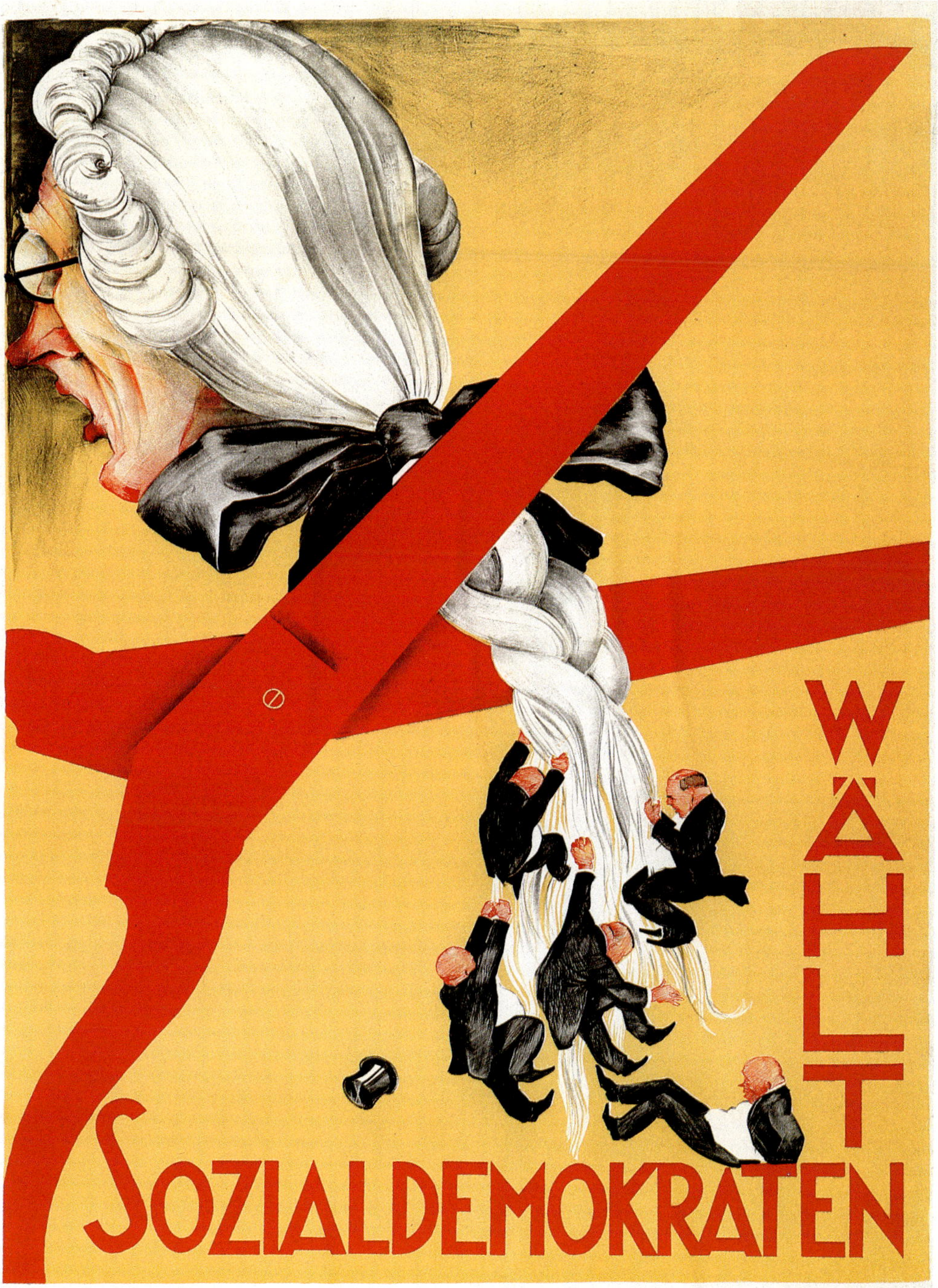

21 **Wählt Sozialdemokraten**
Vote Social Democrats
ca. 1925

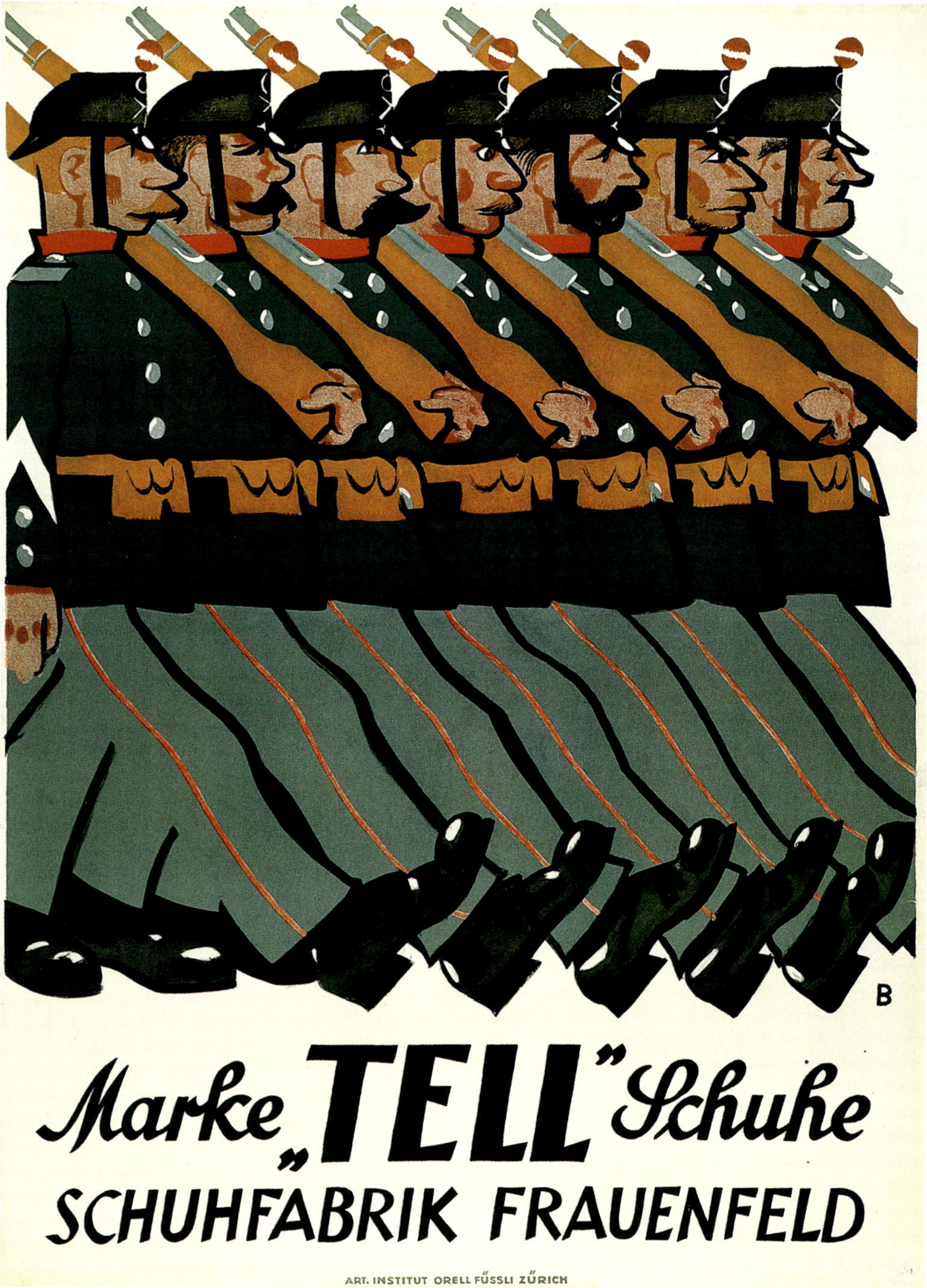

22 **Marke «Tell» Schuhe**
"Tell" brand shoes
1924

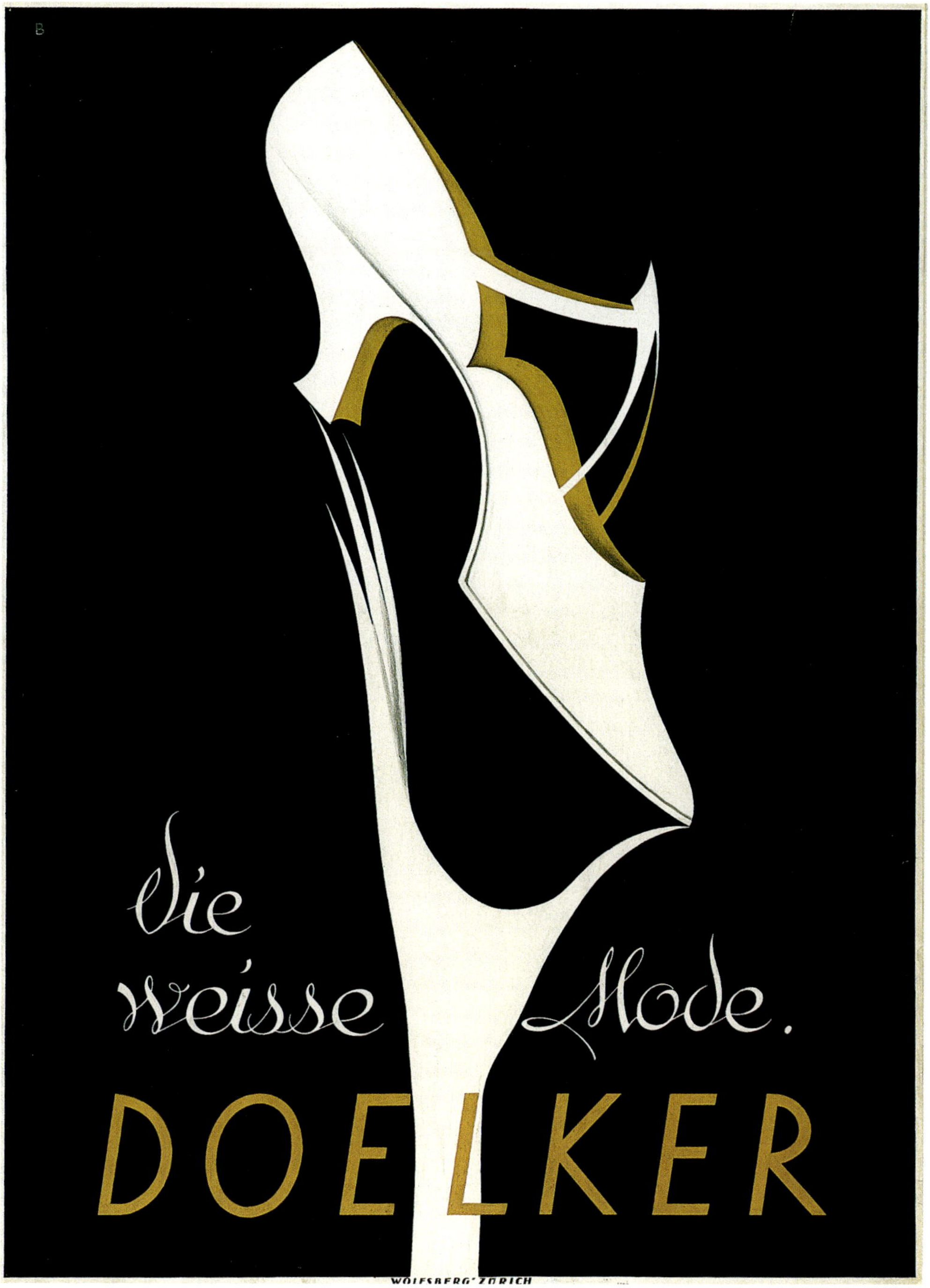

23 **Die weisse Mode. Doelker**
The white fashion. Doelker
1923

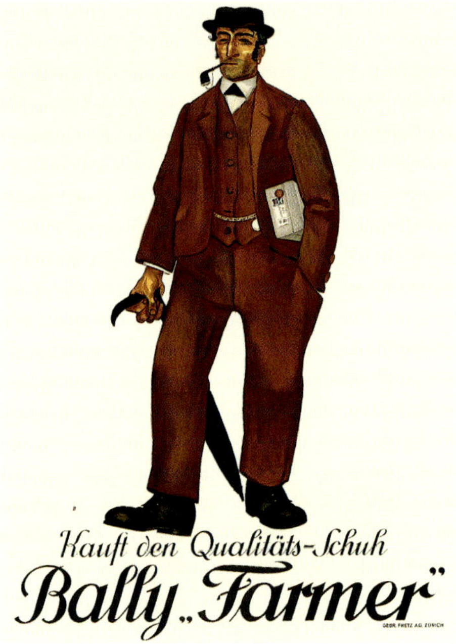

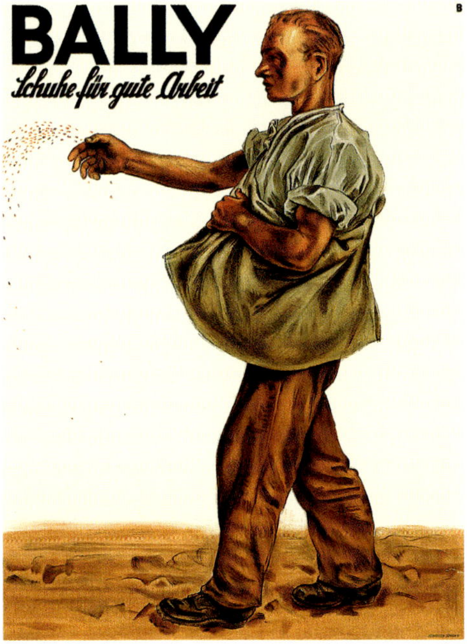

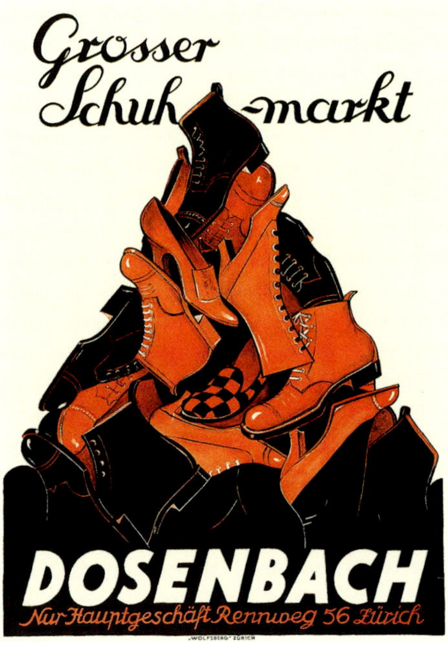

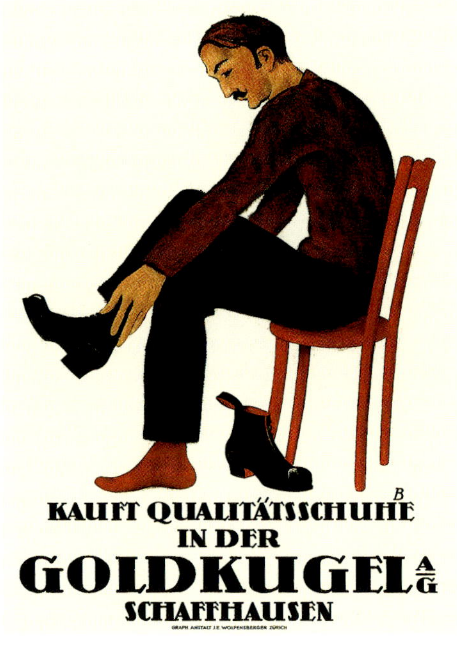

24 **Kauft den Qualitätsschuh Bally «Farmer»**
Buy the Bally "Farmer" quality shoe
1924

25 **Grosser Schuhmarkt / Dosenbach**
Mega shoe store / Dosenbach
ca. 1920

26 **Bally / Schuhe für gute Arbeit**
Bally / Shoes for good work
1934

27 **Kauft Qualitätsschuhe in der Goldkugel Schaffhausen – Buy quality shoes at Goldkugel Schaffhausen**
1920

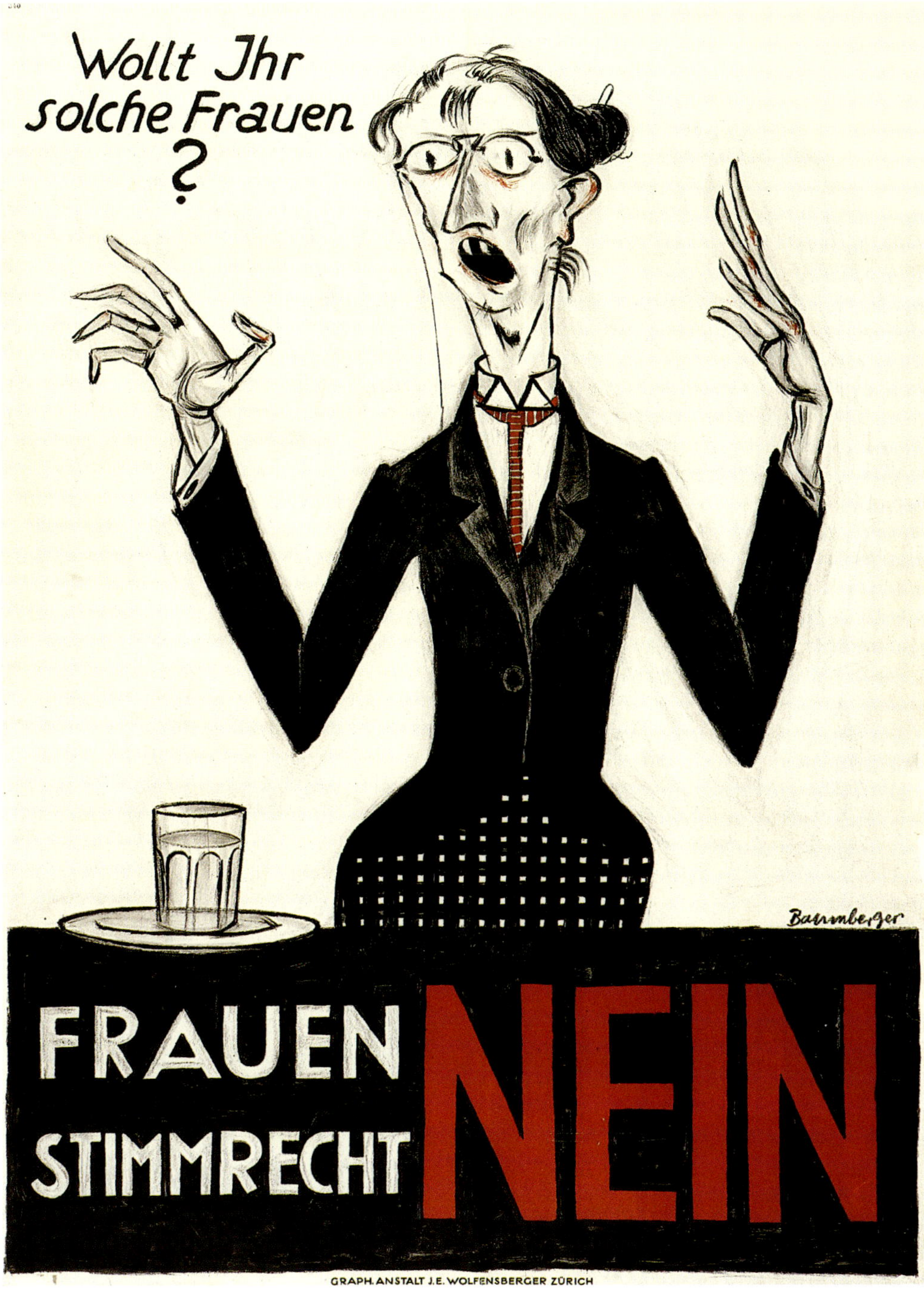

28 **Wollt Ihr solche Frauen? Frauenstimmrecht Nein**
Do you want women like this? No to women's suffrage
1920

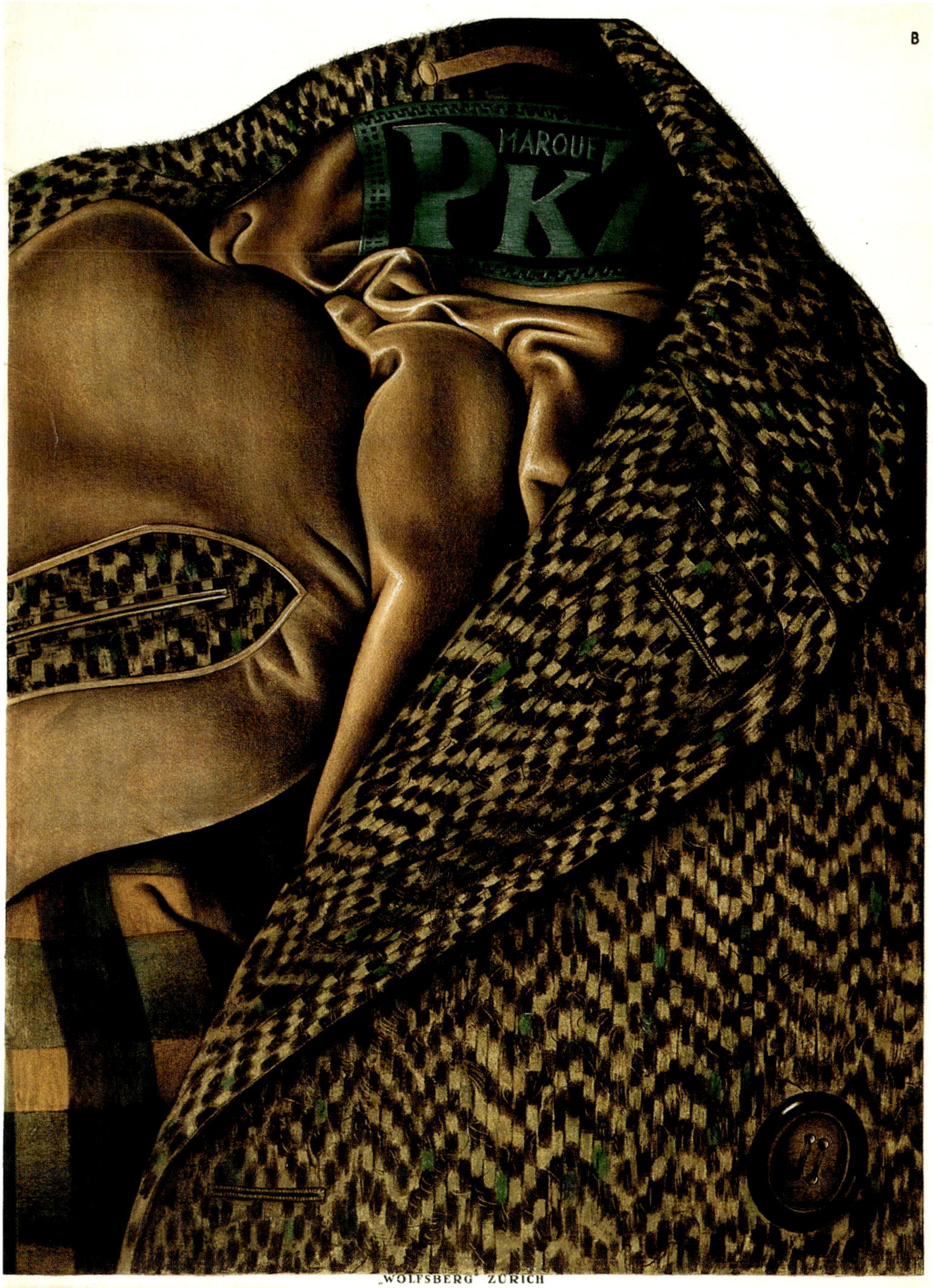

29 **Marque PKZ**
1923

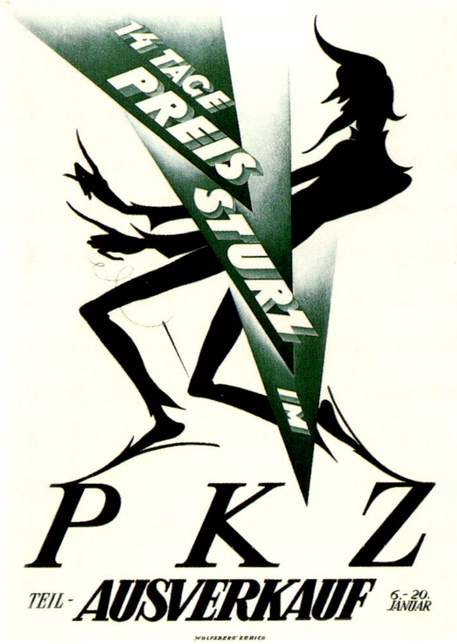

30 **14 Tage Preissturz im PKZ**
14 days of falling prices at the PKZ
1923

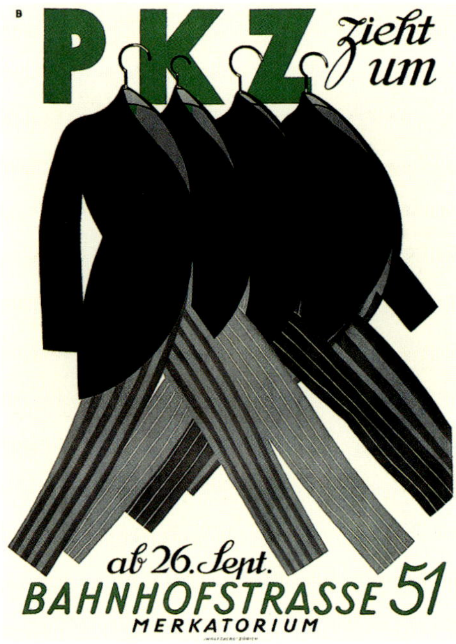

31 **PKZ zieht um**
PKZ is moving
1925

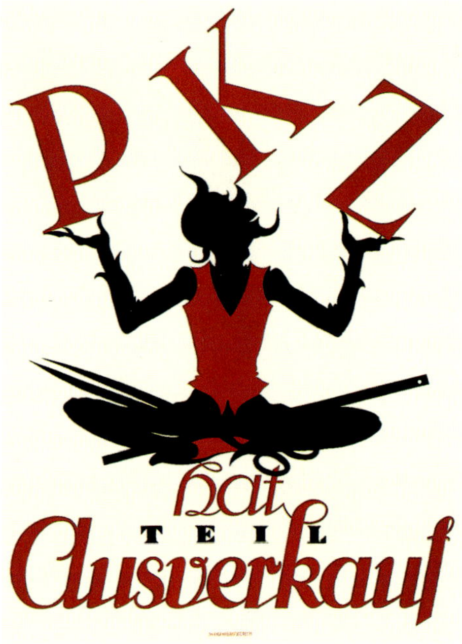

32 **PKZ hat Teilausverkauf**
Sales at PKZ
1922

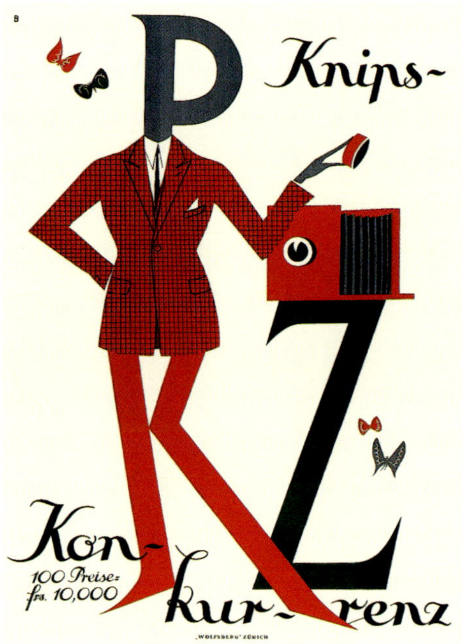

33 **PKZ / Knips-Konkurrenz**
PKZ / Snapshot competition
1923

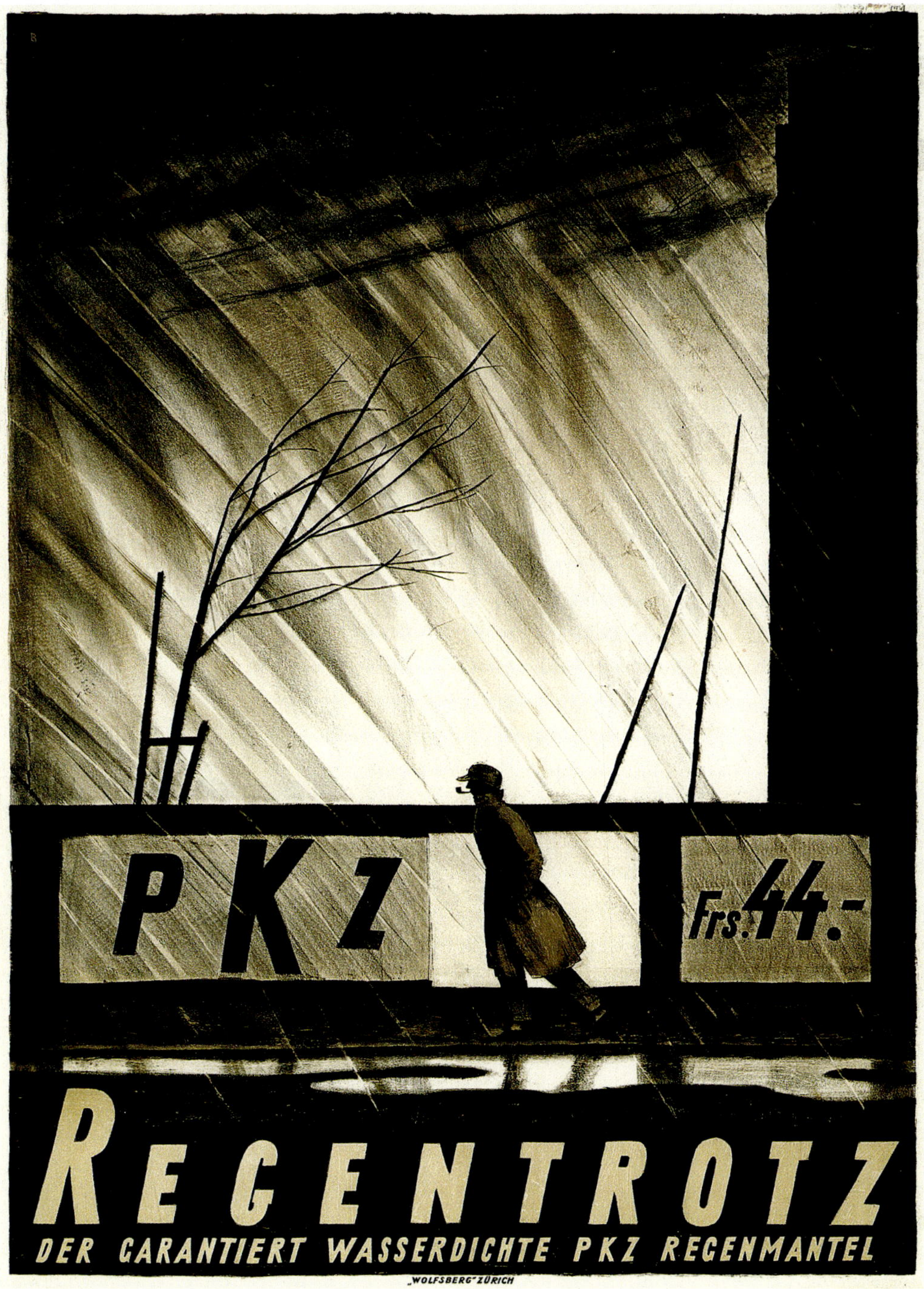

34 **PKZ / Regentrotz**
PKZ / Rain-resister
1924

A STREAMING HISTORY

Martin Heller

It is said that you can never step into the same river twice. Perhaps. But one thing is certain: your feet will get wet each time.

In 1988, I curated an Otto Baumberger exhibition for the Museum für Gestaltung Zürich. The accompanying catalogue proposed to summon up the extensive production of the poster designer in a comprehensive list of works, examining it in essays from various points of view and with extensive graphic examples.[1]

Twenty years later, I have been invited to revisit this body of work, to read and interpret it as a part of advertising and poster art history–and as a pictorial universe.

How is this supposed to work? I remember my earlier approach. I remember my astonishment at the wealth of images and the diversity of artistic languages Baumberger had at his disposal–the dramatic posturing and the visual buffoonery, the pathos of the crude caricatures or folksy veneration of nature. I also remember my ambivalence about a personality that was undoubtedly grand but at the same time incredibly needy, a personality whose inner conflicts were often expressed in a barely-tolerable maudlin sentimentality, yet capable of reaching incredible creative heights.

Bruno Haldner, then Director of the Design Museum of Basel, said–appropriately enough, at an opening–that Otto Baumberger is the Robert de Niro of the Swiss poster: an inconspicuous master of transformation whose identity requires professional role-playing in order to articulate itself.

LIFE IN THE WORK

Re-reading a life and a body of work is a strange experience. The river I see before me does not seem to have changed. It winds its way steadfastly through the early-twentieth-century Swiss cultural landscape, even managing to assert artistic freedom in spots where the banks don't seem to permit. Baumberger's virtuosity still glitters on the surface, and in the depths we can see the bobbing shape of his regret about the consumer world whose products and needs he served so successfully.

Clearly my first encounter with this work had made a lasting impression. Baumberger had been weighed on the scales and found to be sufficiently heavy. And so the result emerged in the form of a biographically inspired analysis that delivered not so much a heroic epic as evidence of a constant struggle to find meaning and quality. So there is no reason to question my earlier assessment. ***Marque PKZ*** 29, ***Baumann***

Bahnhofstr. 25 7, or ***Fein-Kaller*** 52 **are still unbeatable, emblematic masterpieces of brand marketing and discreet seduction.**

Yet, while milestones may mark the path, they scarcely help to explain it; and less still help us understand why this path was taken in the first place. Perception requires empathy. Dipping your toe in the water won't help you see any better, but the experience is there. In touch with the river, sensuality draws us in.

Trying to get closer still, I come across two passages from Baumberger's notes in the 1988 catalogue. I had explored this copious material very carefully at the time, looking for possible interpretations of the artist's desires, which could be sensed in various ways. I remembered both quotations, but suddenly they seemed to be drawn together as though by magnets.

I read: "When painting a landscape it is wonderful to wander about like a little god. Making a winter landscape into a promise of spring, the snowfield receding and conjuring up the wet, sleeping grass and the steaming soil between them in great gray-green and dark brown patches."

And: "It is hardly worthy fighting against anything–except yourself."

A very strange pairing: anyone who thinks in this way expels himself from paradise. Incapable of taking his creative strength seriously as it would bring him too much pleasure, he posits the deficits of a subjective existence as the only valid reality. His language betrays him: the comfort of inventing the world on canvas contrasts with the excessive gesture of moralistic self-accusation.

SWISS TALES

I left the museum world ten years ago. After, certain matters lost importance. For example, the subtleties of art-history discourse that attempts to understand "artistic" and "functional" posters within their respective fields. Or the discussions in Baumberger's day about the new theory and practice of advertising as part of a commodity aesthetic that was giving Modernism an everyday face. I lost touch with such specialized questions as they were replaced by other interests.

For example, as time passes I grow more interested in the stories posters tell. Obviously they are intended to sell things, but what does a poster tell us about its commercial purpose? About the conditions under which it was produced? In other words, about the processes that have brought these particular images into being, and about a culture outside of creative autonomy that they want to and must serve–principally products, naturally, but producers and consumers as well.

And origin is also subject to these kinds of conditions. Twenty years ago I wrote that Otto Baumberger was a Swiss graphic artist. There is a tangibly Swiss quality about his work, hardly ever showing signs of wanting to move outside the nation's borders. Products, motifs, protagonists, and even the folksy, oftentimes course wit of these posters is Swiss through and through.

This Swiss quality strikes me, particularly after the experience I had not had twenty years earlier. The task of giving a profile and a sense of content to the Swiss National Exhibition as artistic director of Expo.02 was my second socialization in terms of a national character. It clarified for me what the Swiss mentality meant on the threshold of the twenty-first century. And without intending to pursue every detail of the ramifications of this learning period, it is interesting to focus on it here. Determining to what extent someone like Otto Baumberger embodied Switzerland is still very much relevant today, as if it were part of a genetic code.

This code weaves through Baumberger's work as a sort of thematic thread that owes nothing to any particular commission, but rather grows out of the native soil–leitmotifs of an aesthetic and a social orientation that go beyond individual ambition and artistic ability.

SOLIDITY

Solid are the merry, hungry citizens in the Zurich Restaurant du Pont, who having had enough to eat are really quite full 45. Solid is the high-quality Bally "Farmer" shoe as it moves along 24. Solidly brilliant is Otto Baumberger's craft: as a trained lithographer he probably made most of the printing stones himself. Solidly serene are the typefaces as well, without any extravagance, as are the compositions that embrace Art Nouveau, Expressionism, and Cubism. Even the over-the-top, touristy landscapes are so solidly constructed that it seems as though there was a need to convince travelers from home and abroad that nothing occurs here that is not genuine or just 90. It is as though the safe footsteps and the even breathe of our nation can be heard in Otto Baumberger's posters. Conversely, no one shows any lack of solidity or acts frivolously here–that would not go well in the land of self-righteousness, even under the conditions of globalization.

URBANSCAPE

Urbanscape Switzerland is part of current discourse. It attempts to define a territory that still boasts of the traditional contrast between city and country, but in reality has long been comprised of a complex structure of predominantly part-urban, part-suburban conurbations. Here Baumberger's posters provide an unexpected commentary upon an earlier, almost anachronistic period: rural and urban Switzerland are fused to project a rather coherent pictorial quality 93. It is true, however, that the consumer worlds are directed at diverse publics. But, on the one hand, the range in between them is diffuse, and on the other there is a basic tonality of a discrete idyll in Baumberger's poster Switzerland, an idyll that is just as accessible to the elegant urbanity as to the impregnable rurality.

NEUTRALITY

Of course we are not talking about the political doctrine of neutrality here. What is much more striking is that the images Baumberger creates are impregnated to a certain extent with the fact that nothing is ever really taken too seriously in Switzerland. Even when political conflict seems to be flaring up, Baumberger effortlessly changes not only styles but sides as well 20, 21. Or when military aircraft fly just for the viewing public 66, and masked balls are not just occasions of opulent festivity, but mere masquerades 17. Or when there might be a sense that Baumberger's often cerebral, perhaps unreal or, literally, "poster" people could keep themselves at a distance from world events and remain incapable of acting. Neutrality is in the air as a social virtue and as a latent readiness to beat an unduly rapid retreat from anything that just might get out of control.

FOREIGNNESS

How much foreignness can Switzerland bare? Otto Baumberger's Steinfels pictures are alien–illustrative views of the world for pasting into collector's albums 63, 80. Or the Orient, which offers its services through such products as cigarettes, soap, fountain pens, textiles, or carpets 13. Or the animals in the Zurich Zoo, four-legged or feathered friends from around the world 69. Or what about the promises of cinematographers, whose screen is the canvas for projecting anything that happens beyond the Swiss border 64. Of course this clear distinction between what is our own and what is alien is obsolete in today's Switzerland. But it still does define part of a self-image that is extremely popular, and one that awakens certain longings that serve as potential political capital. Alien things are welcome, so long as they are colorful, mysterious, touching, distanced–in other words, exotica. If this exoticism is missing, then the images are no longer convincing. Unless it is to denounce the alien quality in something that is our own–for example those monstrous women demanding equal rights 28.

FEAR

There are no beaming smiles in Baumberger's posters, no basic undercurrent of cheerfulness: fear is the key. There is rarely a face, full of fear, like that of the city policeman, who can be called by dialing 17 47. Or perhaps it is better not to. The fact is that not much separates assistance from punishment. Much more often the fear is simply there, sitting in people's eyes, disguising itself as despondency or darkness, protecting the Swiss cross from receiving undue attention 79, or not having the confidence to live out the pleasure of doing or seeing. And we remember: no conflict, as it is scarcely worth it–unless it is conflict with yourself. It is this primal fear and self-doubt that the right wing has served up in recent years, in an entirely unspeakable fashion, by appealing to the majority–or at least to their own clientele. This fear and doubt is a Swiss raw material, effortlessly renewing itself for decades.

THE BOUNDARIES OF INTERPRETABILITY

So I have got my feet wet. Of course Otto Baumberger's world is not mine. But I can certainly relate to that part of it I experience as I go about my daily life. The life's work of this highly talented artist–who aspired to great inventive heights artistically but instead illustrated what was already there, in his posters and in his art, drawings, and illustration cycles–has drawn nearer to me in a manner quite distinct from my first encounter.

There is a sequence of posters for the Red Cross from 1943 in which Baumberger presents the miseries of war. Hollow-cheeked figures, drawn in shadow, the stereotypical victims of war, represent the thousands. The only motif that can withstand this sort of schematic approach is a self-portrait 71. Baumberger drew himself, with his fifty-four years, as an internee, tired, melancholic, his head in his hands, looking down at the floor. As though there was no outside world any more that could give pleasure to the eye, no space, no purpose.

It seems as though this Otto Baumberger had lost the battle with himself, or had given up, or perhaps never even waged it consistently or in any real way. But can such an image–a mere quotation–suggest an interpretation and assessment that reveals itself in Baumberger's two hundred plus posters.

The fact is that any speculation about Baumberger's self-confidence, his inconsistency or vulnerability, is only possible because there is something within his creative output that leaves him open to attack. In the tendency for certain formulae and creative solutions; in the artistic searching; in the response–often firm but just as often wavering–to the freedoms and constraints of the epoch, to his clients, or to his own ambition.

BEYOND WISHES

At this point I have become aware of another shift of perspective that comes from my second reading. Twenty years ago, the idea of a life's work was a more or less abstract matter as far as I was concerned. It had something to do with the perspective gained from analyzing a substantial quantity of data and material rather than concentrating on individual works. More material raised the prospect of a wider range of possibilities and forms of access. Back then that perception of a higher order was still unknown to me.

I am now fifty-six years old, two years older than Baumberger when he was–perhaps–interned as a result of his own doing, locked up inside himself. But the comparable age engenders sensitivity to a dimension that really is more existential–to questions about the vital weight of an oeuvre, about the meaning and validity of taking stock. And about justifying confidence in that aspect of the world that is much more than a picture story.

Can water age, can a river? Or is it just our feet?

Baumberger designed hardly any more posters after the war. His time, put simply albeit brutally, had past. And teaching at the ETH probably gave him greater financial freedom. Apart from the wide-ranging cycle of illustrations for the Bible and for great works of world literature, until the end of his life in 1961 he produced some 200 abstract compositions, which–as can be seen from German Wikipedia[2]–have remained largely unknown.

1 *Otto Baumberger, 1889–1961*, Reihe Schweizer Plakatgestalter 4, ed. Martin Heller, exh. cat., Museum für Gestaltung Zürich (Zurich 1988).
2 Otto Baumberger's English entry in Wikipedia contains only the place and date of his birth and death, and one external link.

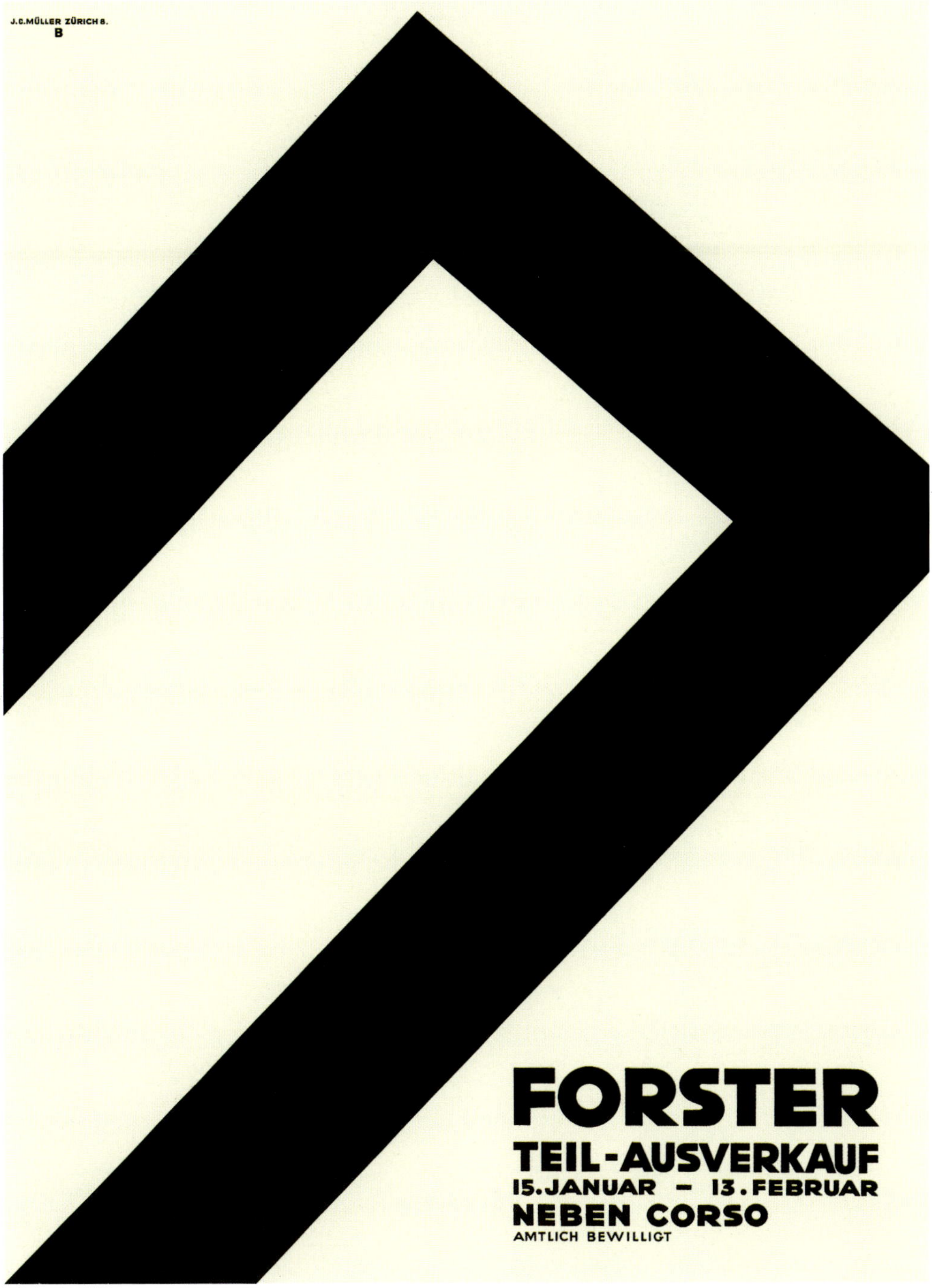

35 **Forster / Teil-Ausverkauf**
Forster / Sales
1930

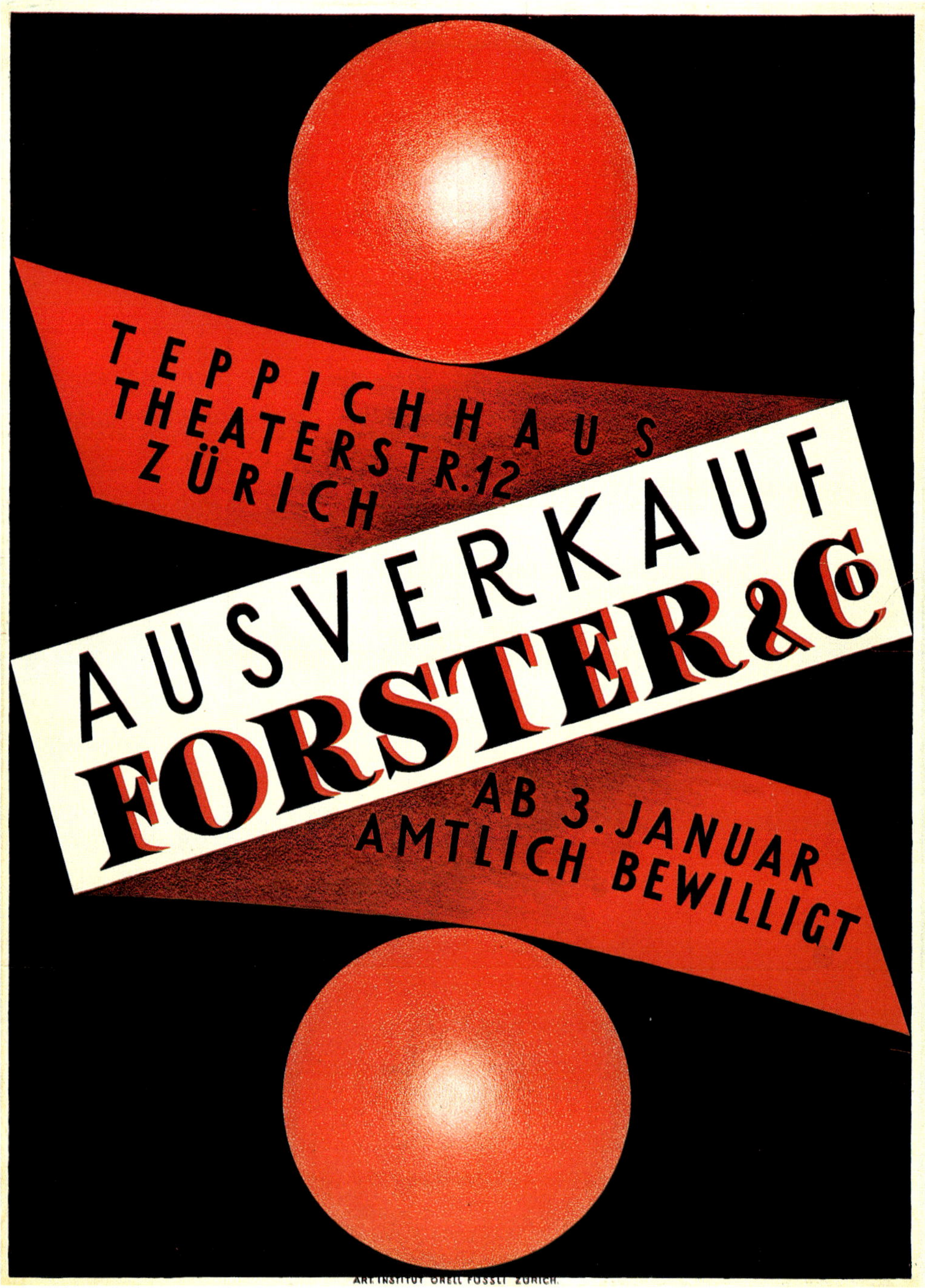

36 **Ausverkauf Forster & Co.**
Forster & Co. sales
1926

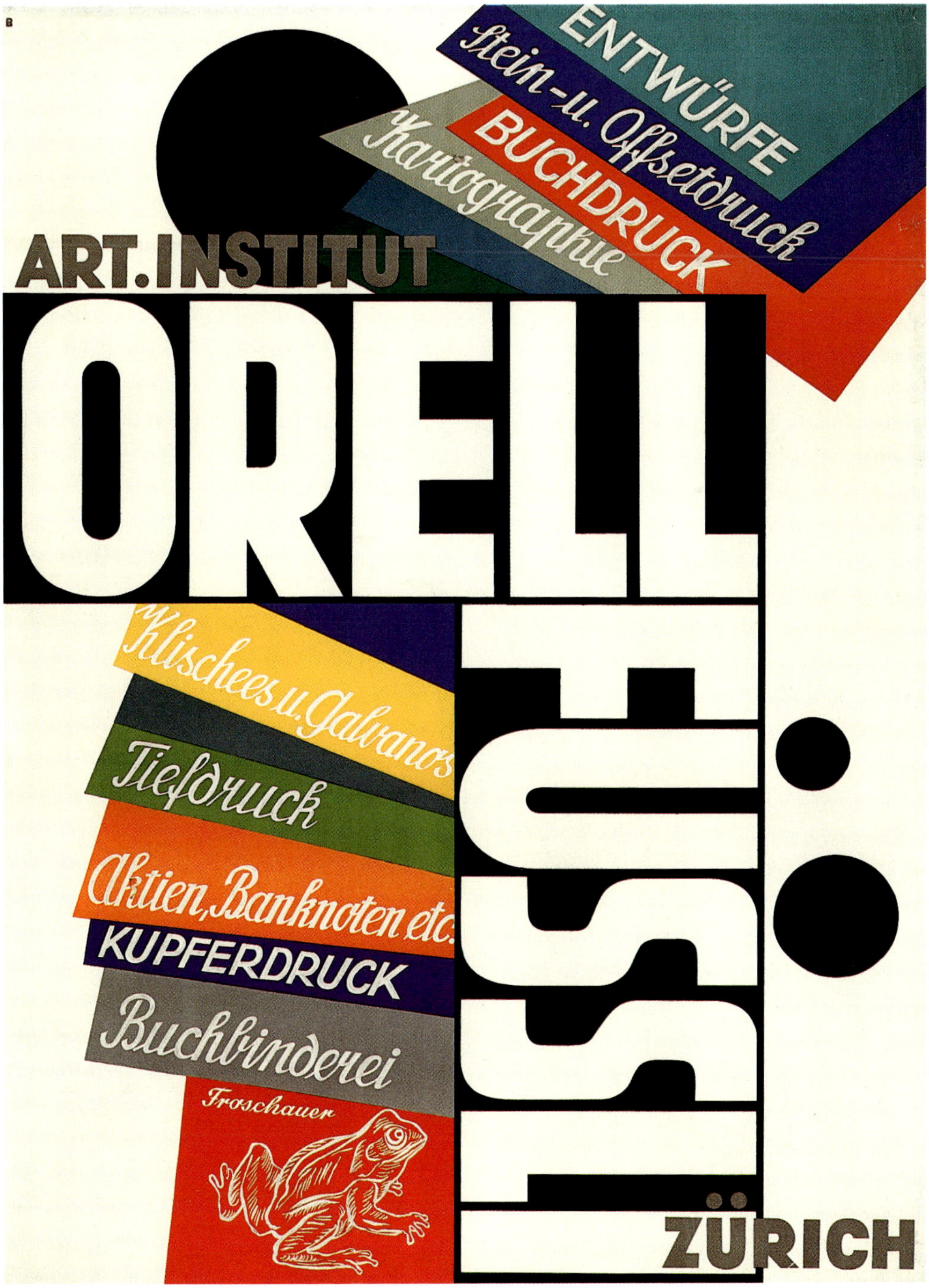

37 **Art. Inst. Orell Füssli Zürich**
1928

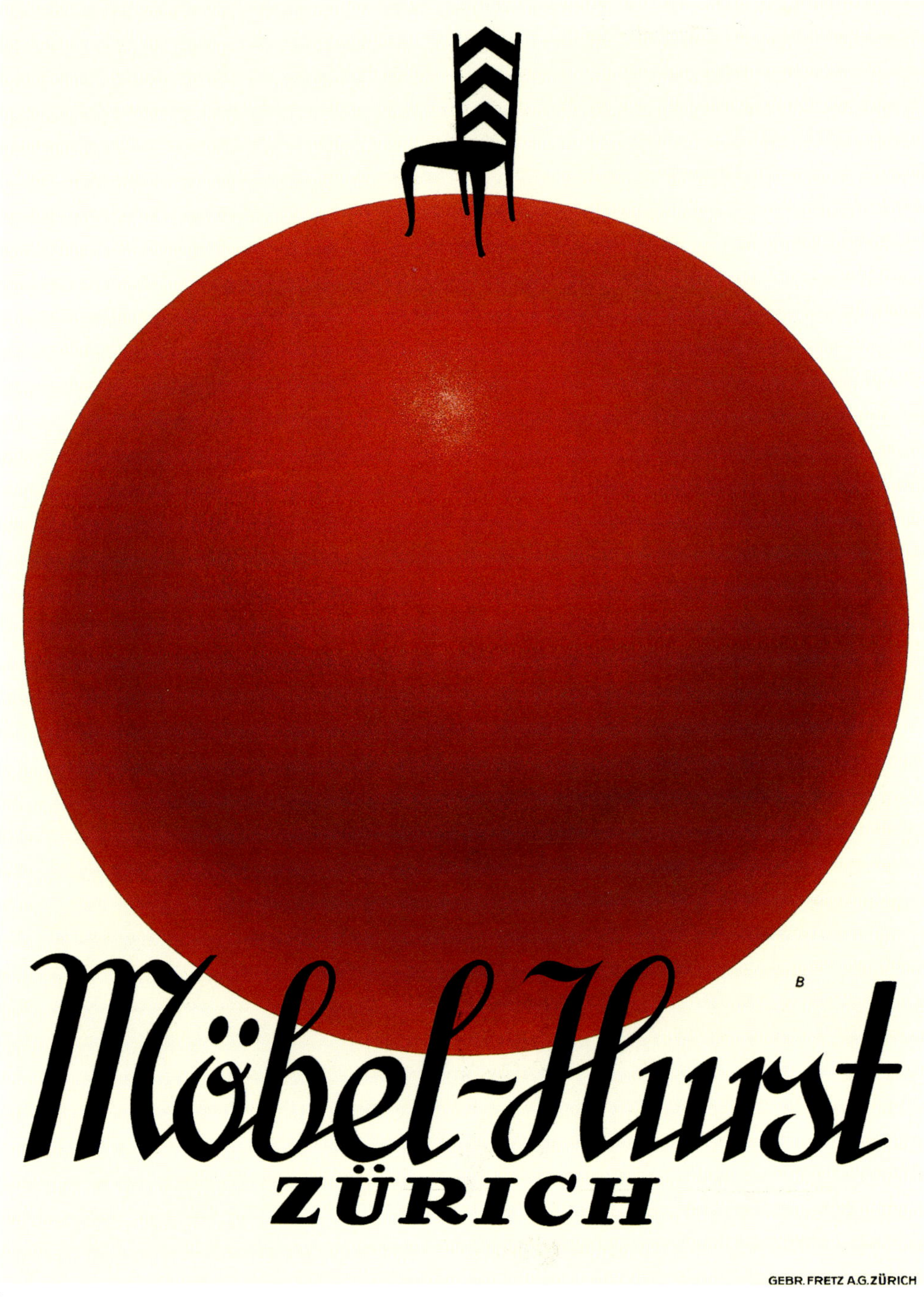

38 **Möbel-Hurst Zürich**
ca. 1924

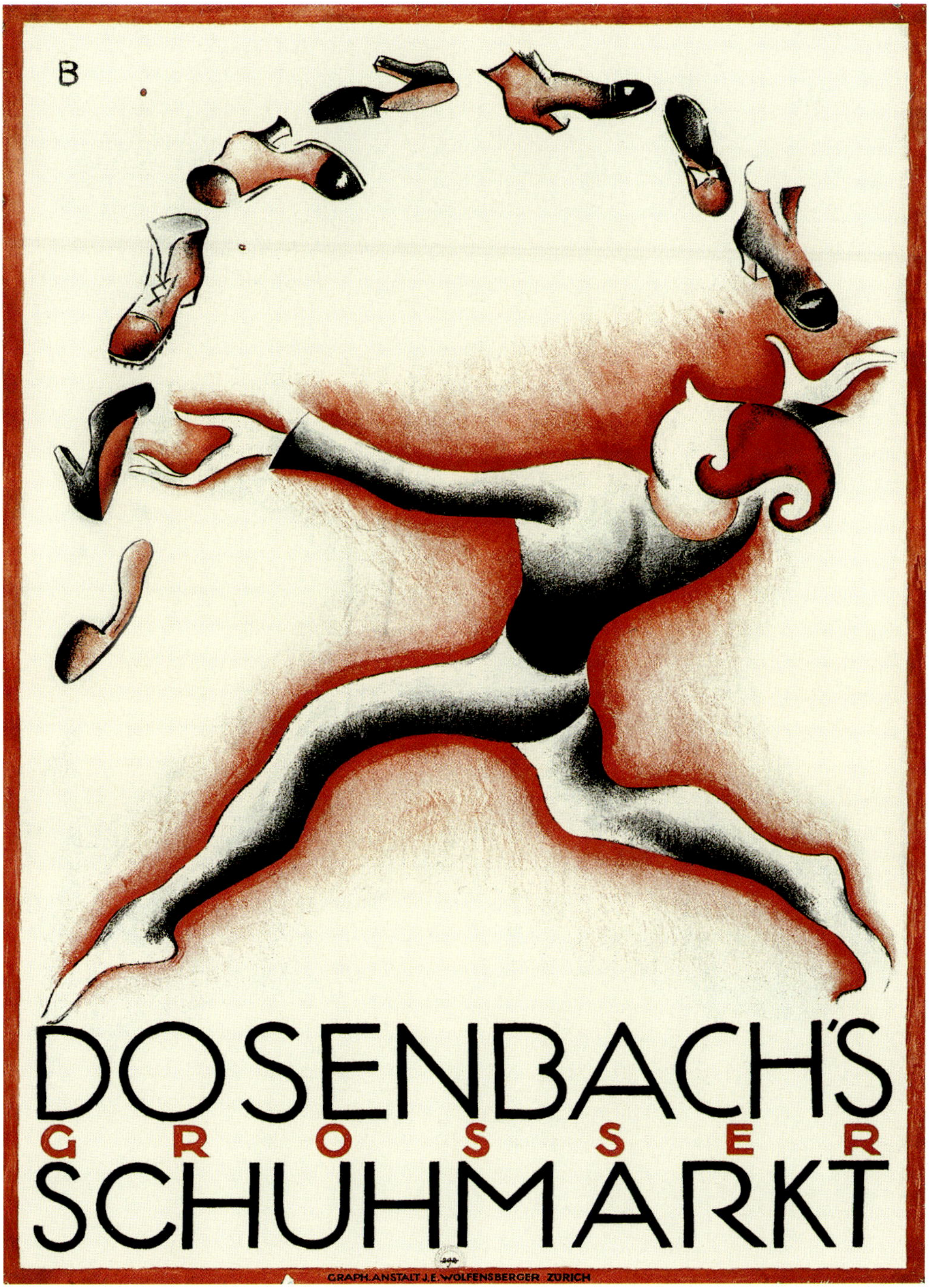

39 **Dosenbach's grosser Schuhmarkt**
Dosenbach's mega shoe store
1915

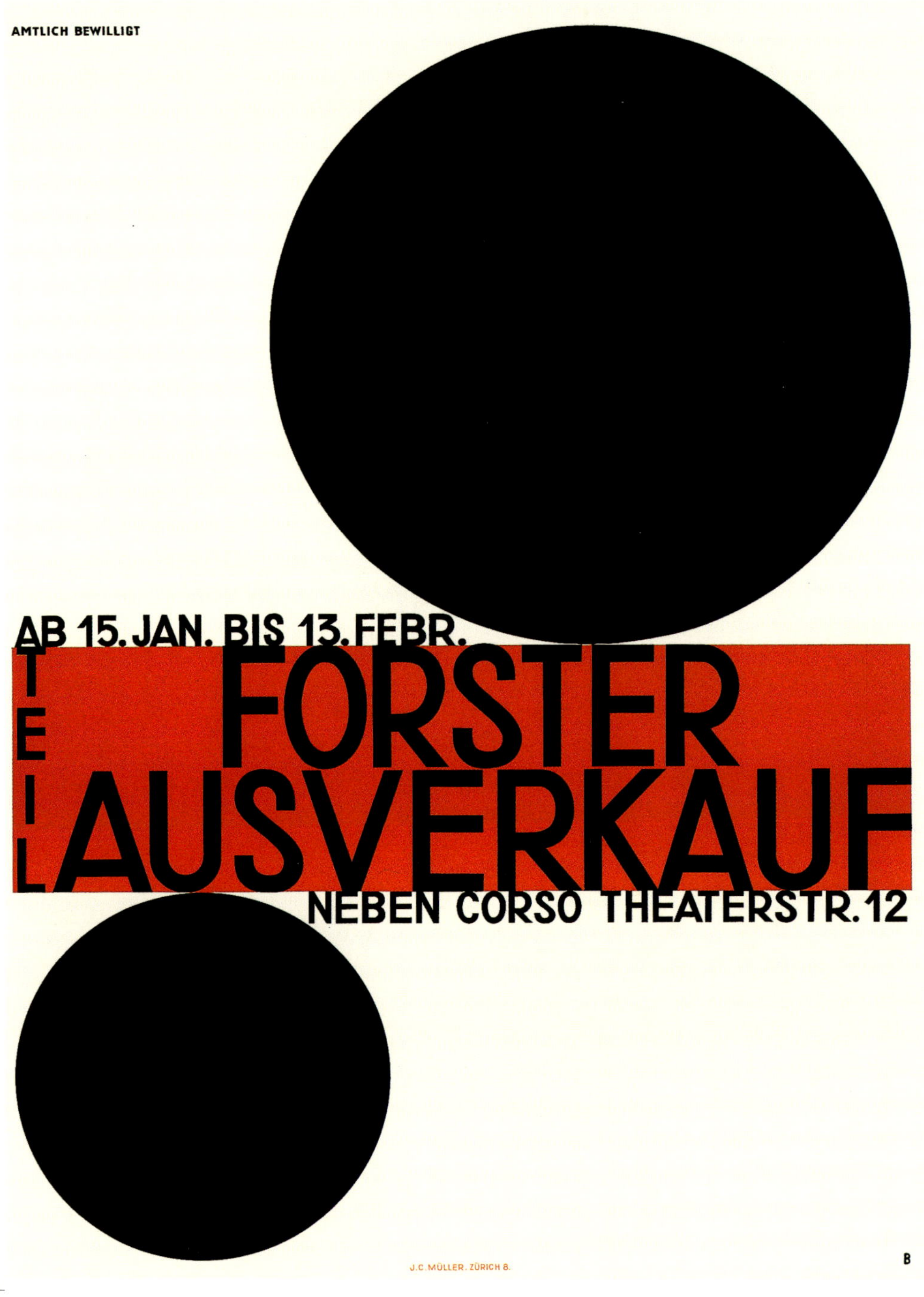

40 **Forster / Teilausverkauf**
Forster / Sales
1928

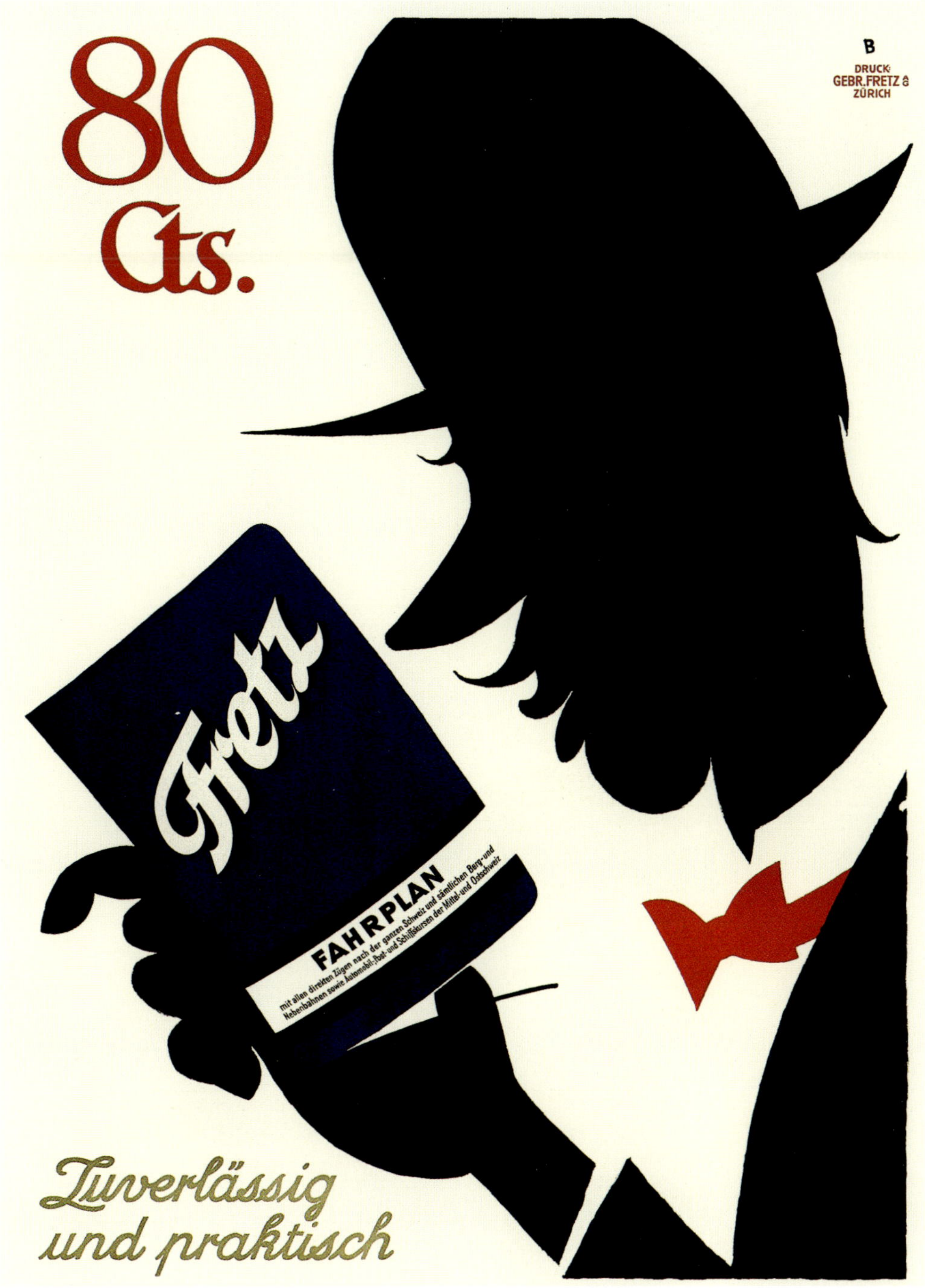

41 **Fretz Fahrplan**
Fretz timetable
1923

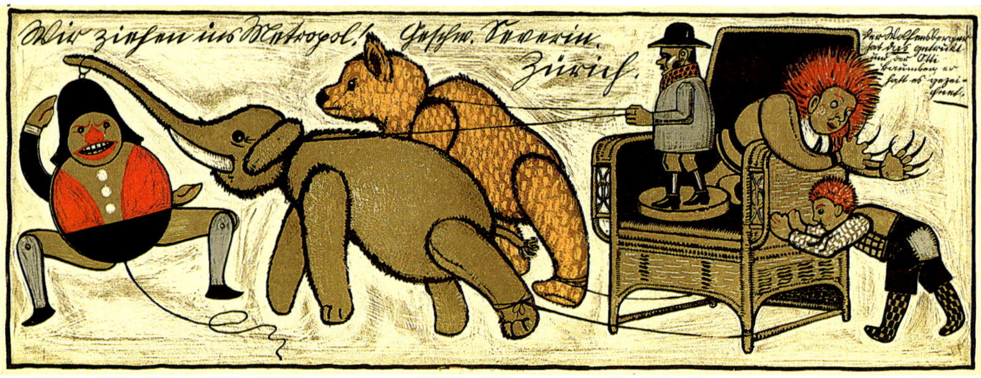

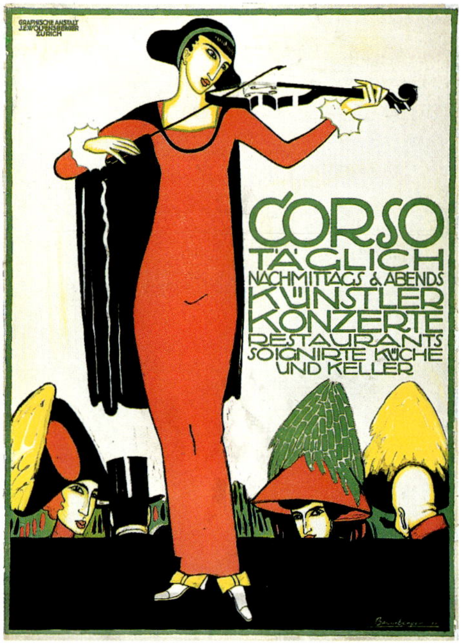

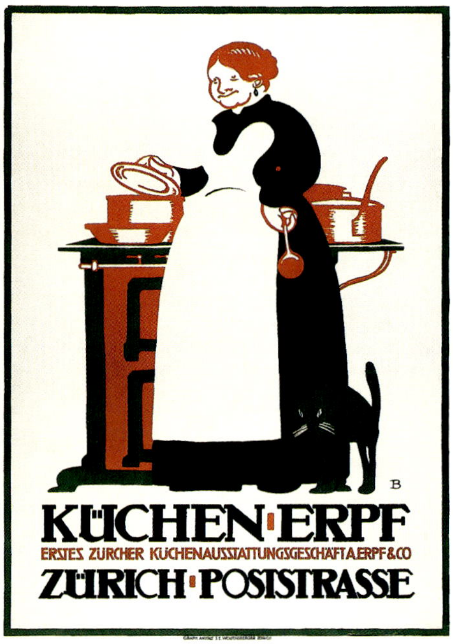

42 **Wir ziehen ins Metropol! Geschw. Severin, Zürich**
We are moving to the Metropol!
1911

43 **Corso / Künstlerkonzerte**
Corso / Artiste concerts
1911

44 **Küchen-Erpf Zürich**
1913

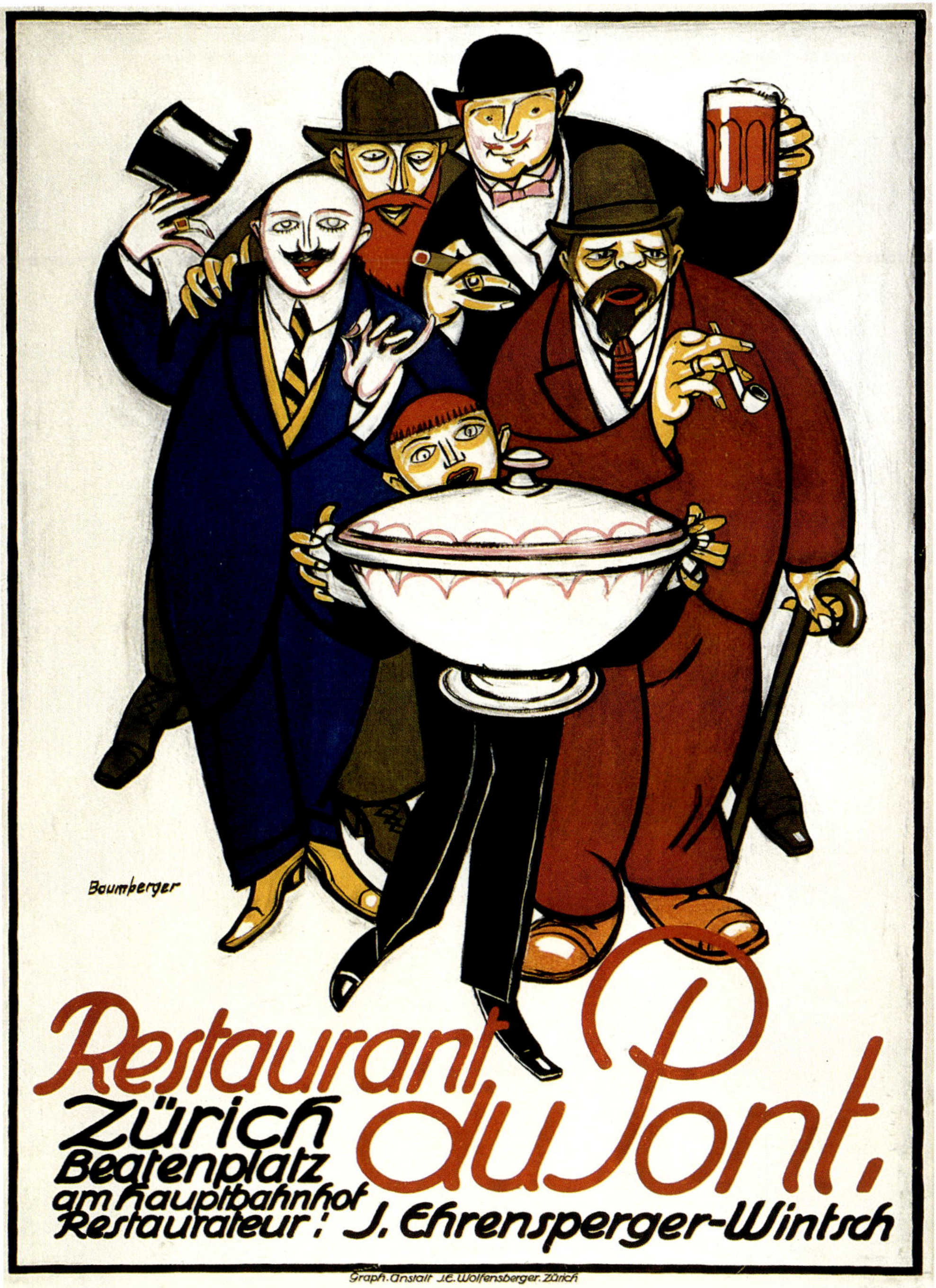

45 **Restaurant du Pont. Zürich**
1913

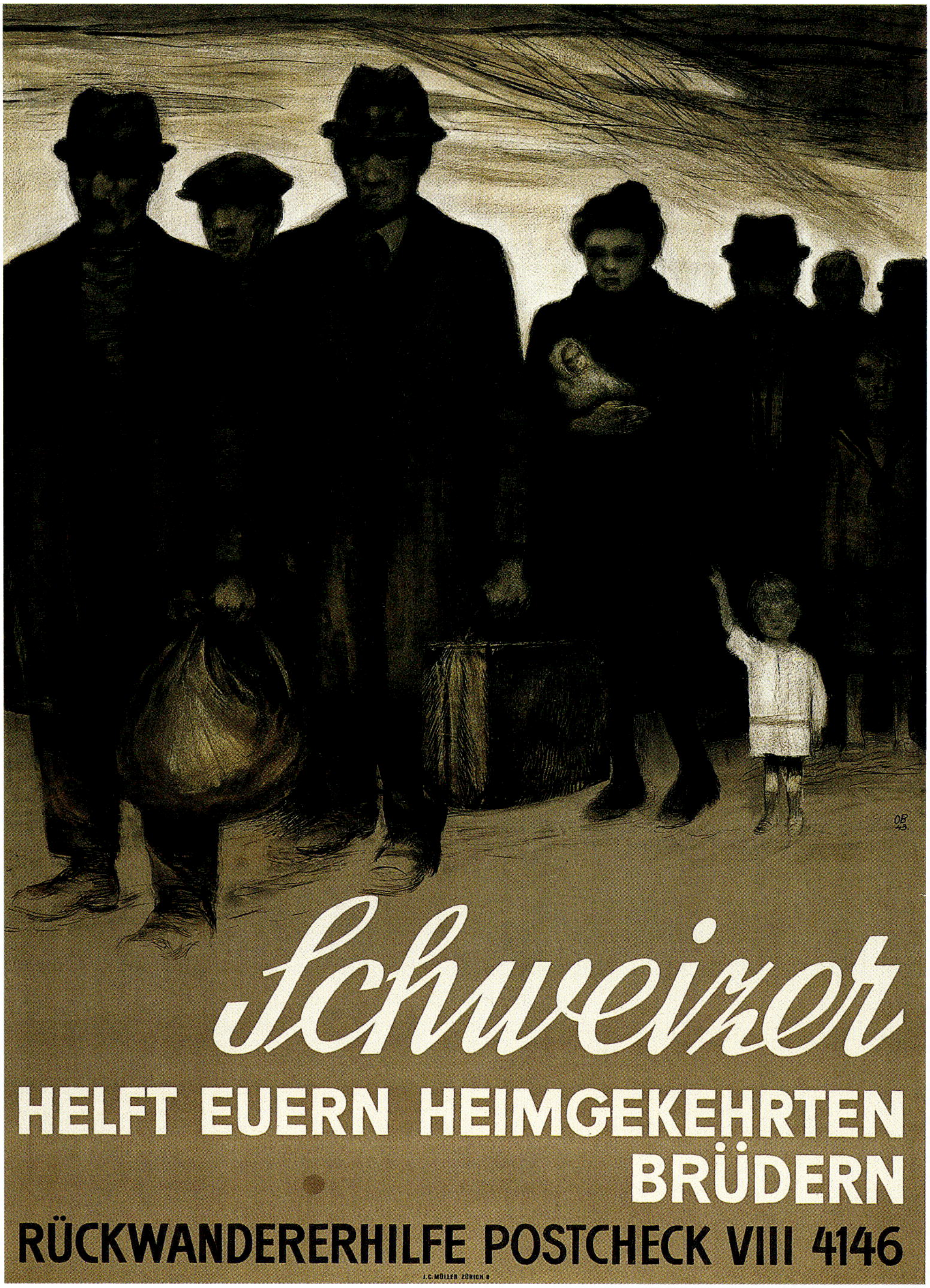

46 **Schweizer / helft euern heimgekehrten Brüdern / Rückwandererhilfe**
Swiss citizens / help your returning brothers / Help with repatriation
1943

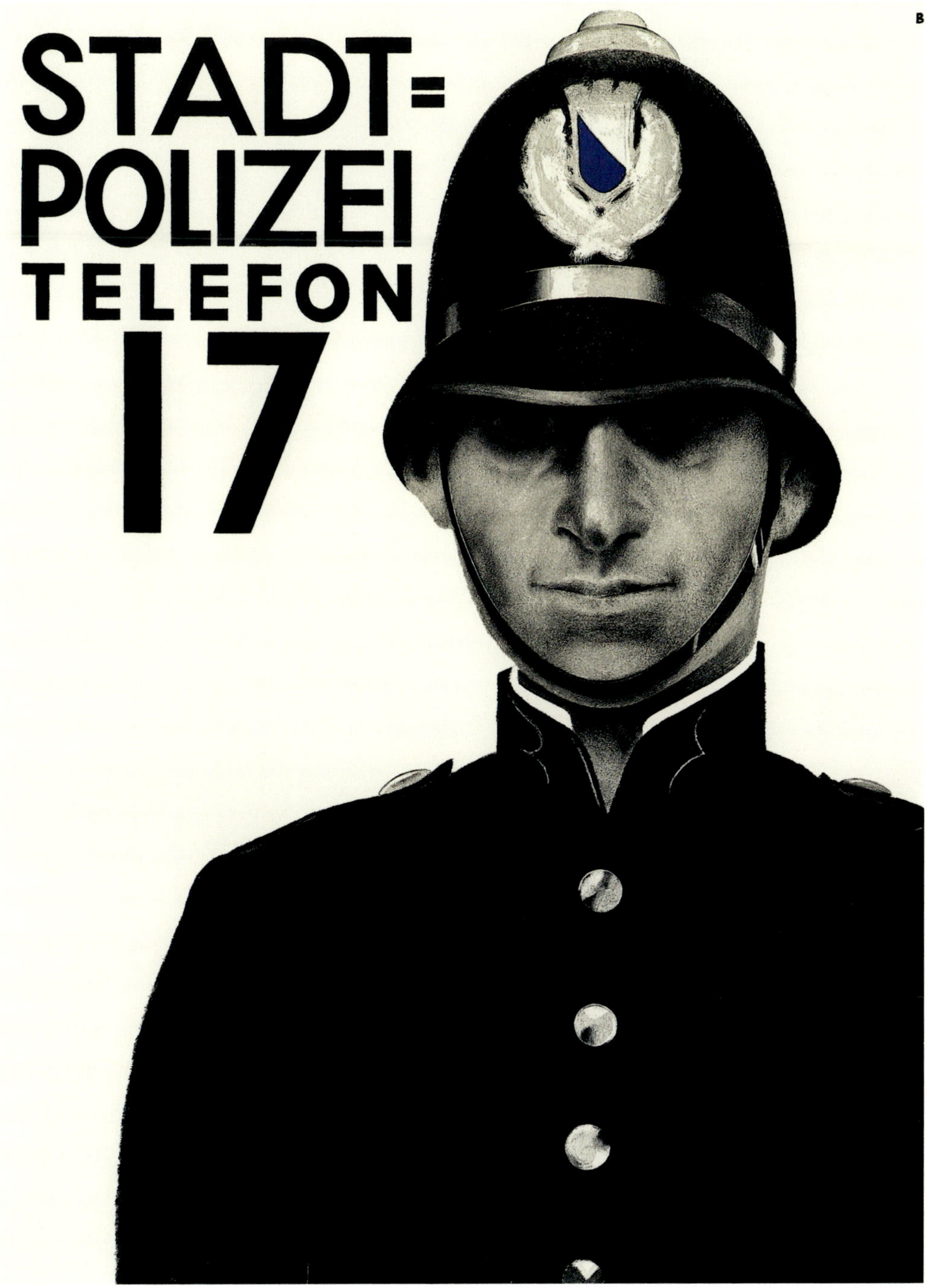

47 **Stadt-Polizei / Telefon 17**
Municipal police / Telephone 17
1931

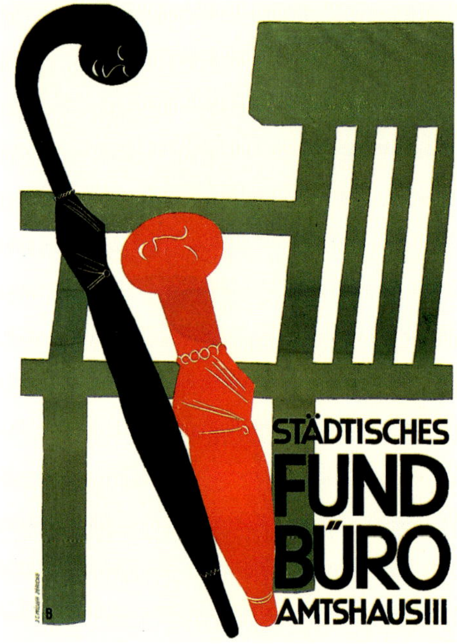

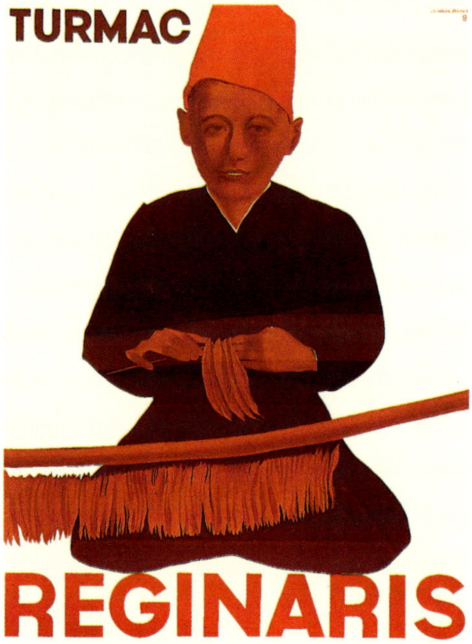

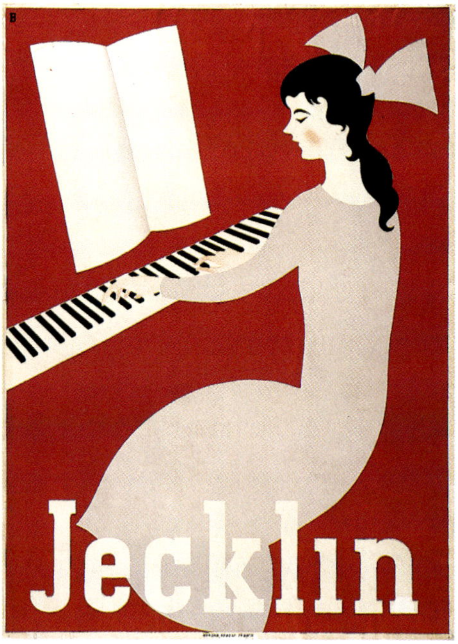

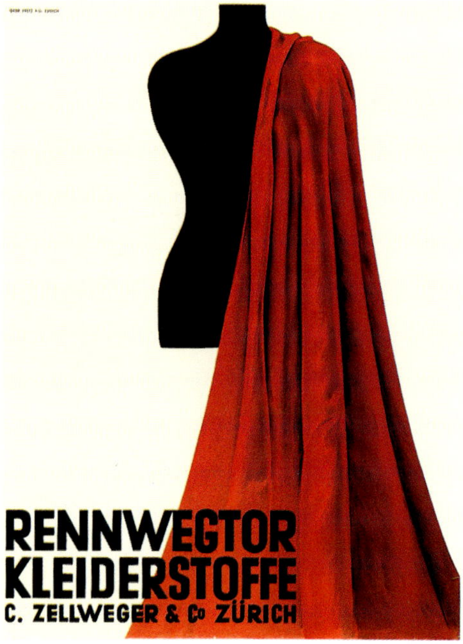

48 **Städtisches Fundbüro**
Municipal lost property office
1931

49 **Jecklin**
1918

50 **Turmac Reginaris**
1933

51 **Rennwegtor Kleiderstoffe / C. Zellweger & Co. Zürich – Rennwegtor dress fabric**
1931

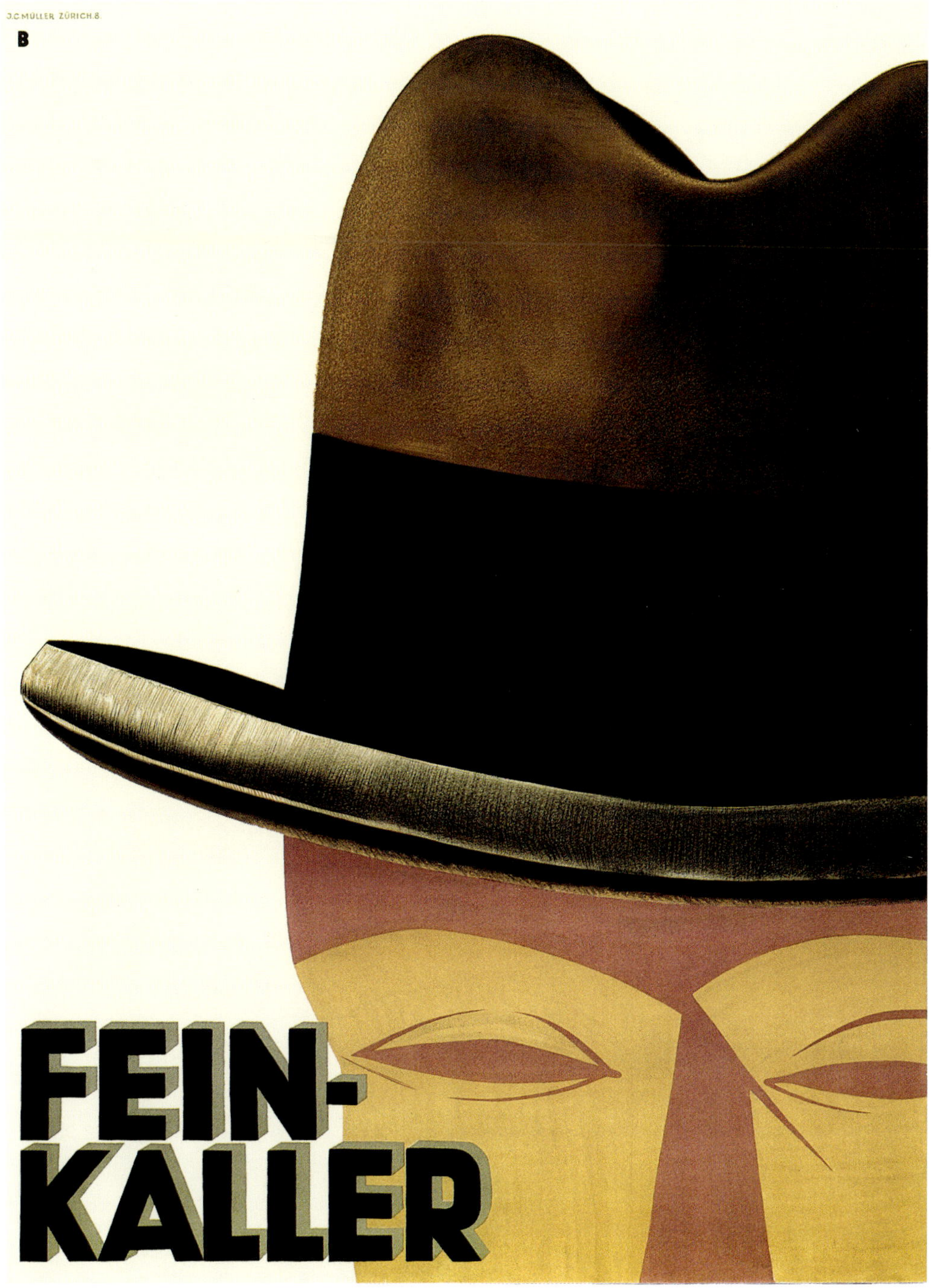

52 **Fein-Kaller**
1930

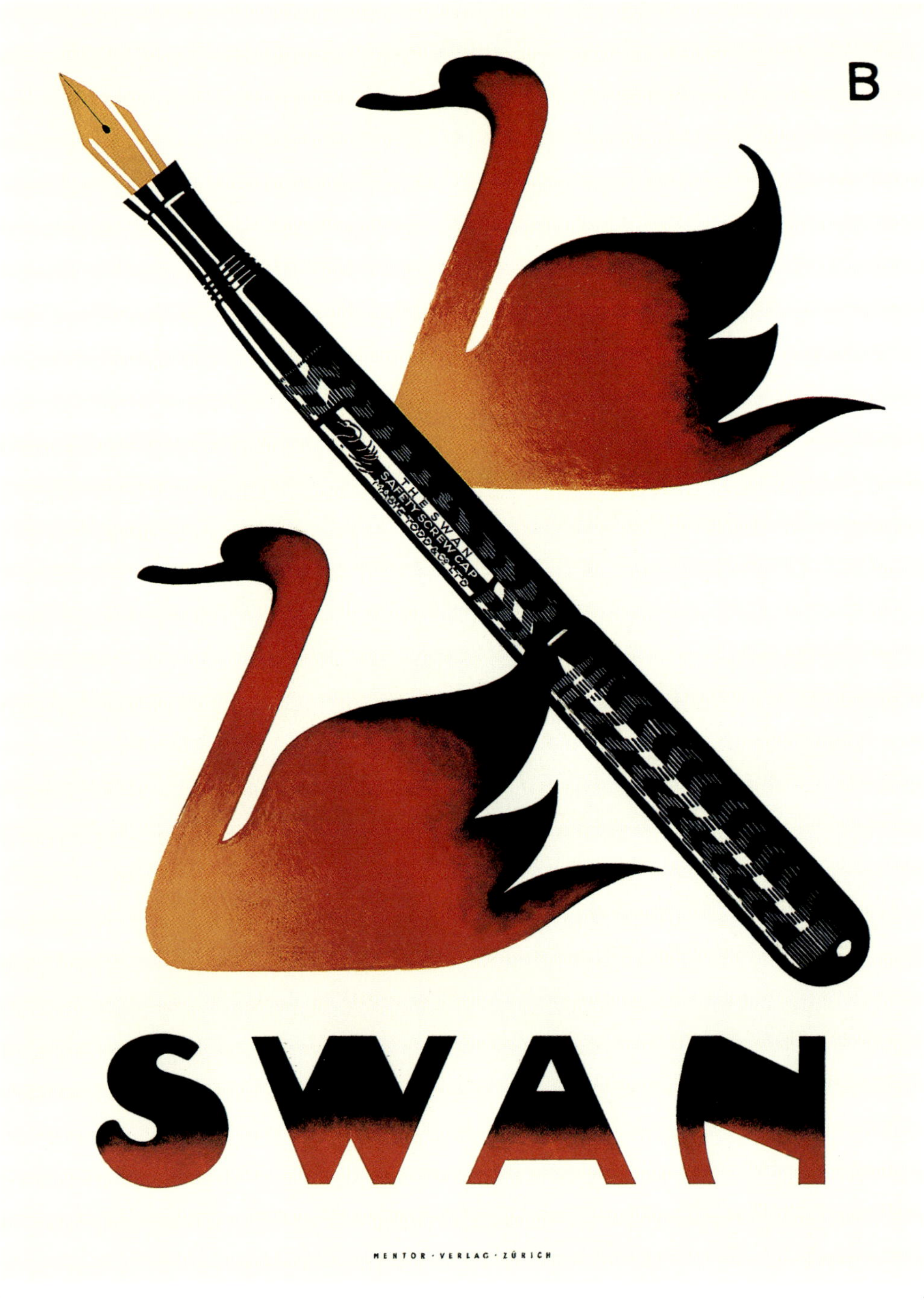

53 **Swan**
1919

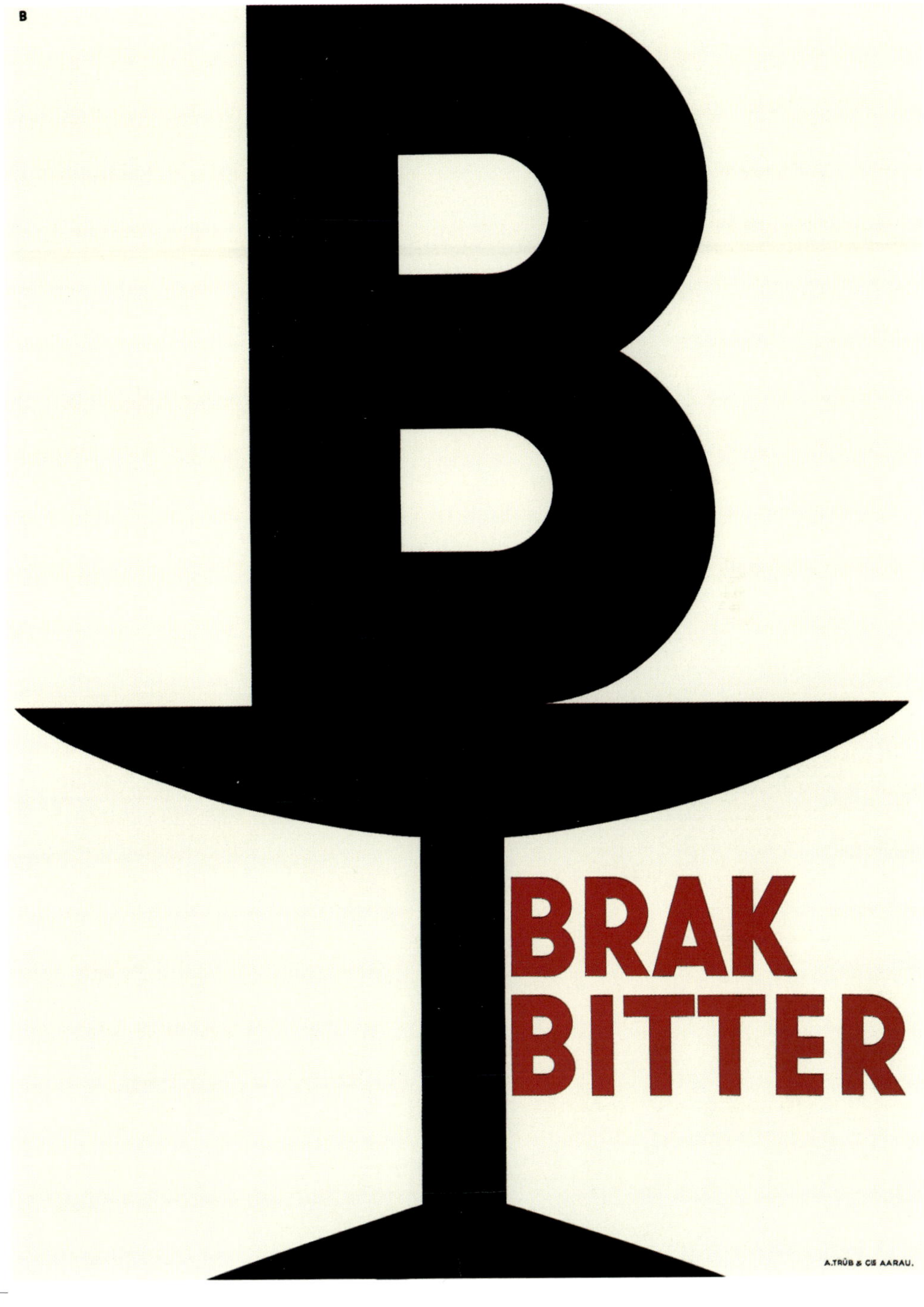

54 **Brak Bitter**
1937

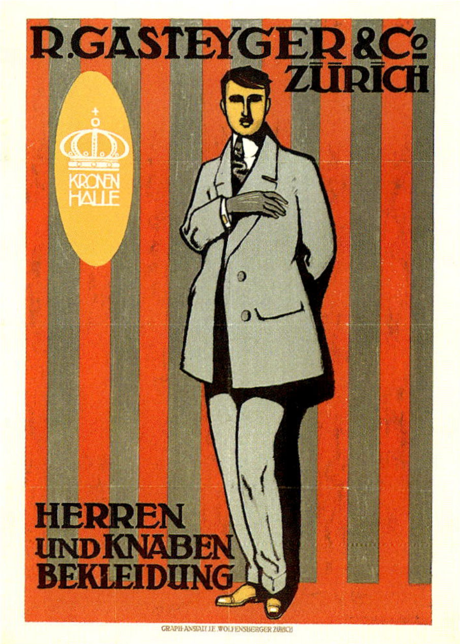

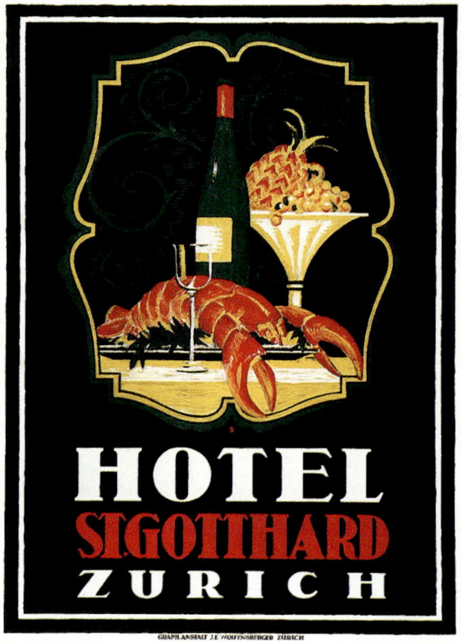

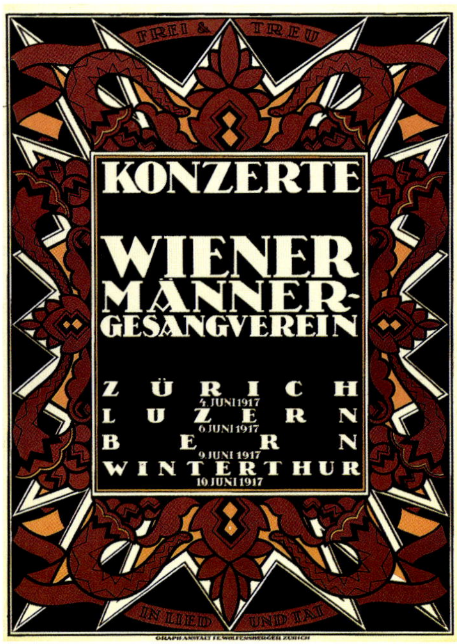

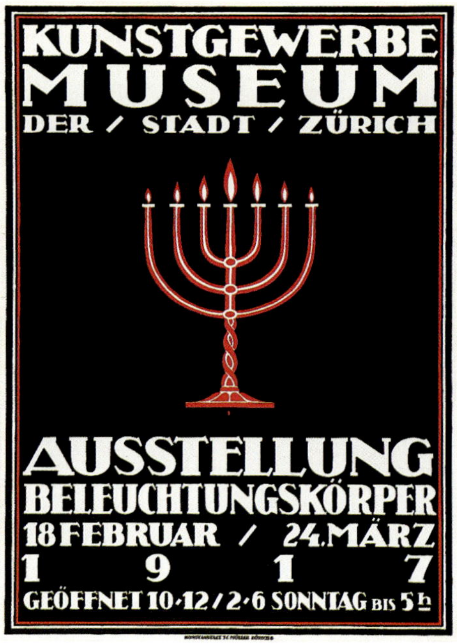

55 **R. Gasteyger & Co. Zürich / Herren und Knaben Bekleidung – Men's and boys' clothing**
1911

56 **Konzerte / Wiener Männergesangsverein Concerts / Vienna Men's Choir**
1917

57 **Hotel St. Gotthard Zürich**
1917

58 **Kunstgewerbemuseum der Stadt Zürich / Ausstellung Beleuchtungskörper – Lighting fixtures exhibit**
1917

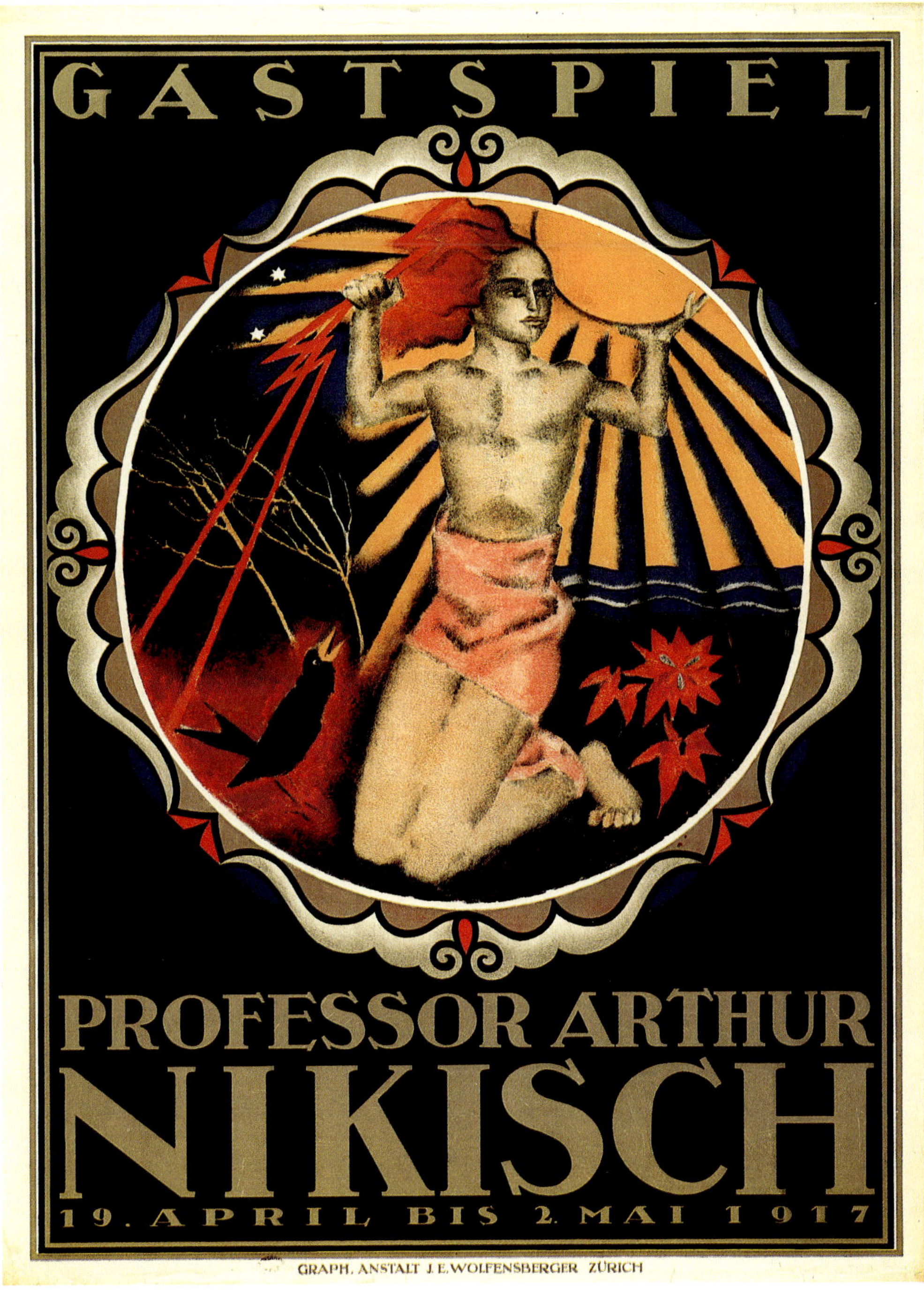

59 **Gastspiel Professor Arthur Nikisch**
Guest performance by Professor Arthur Nikisch
1917

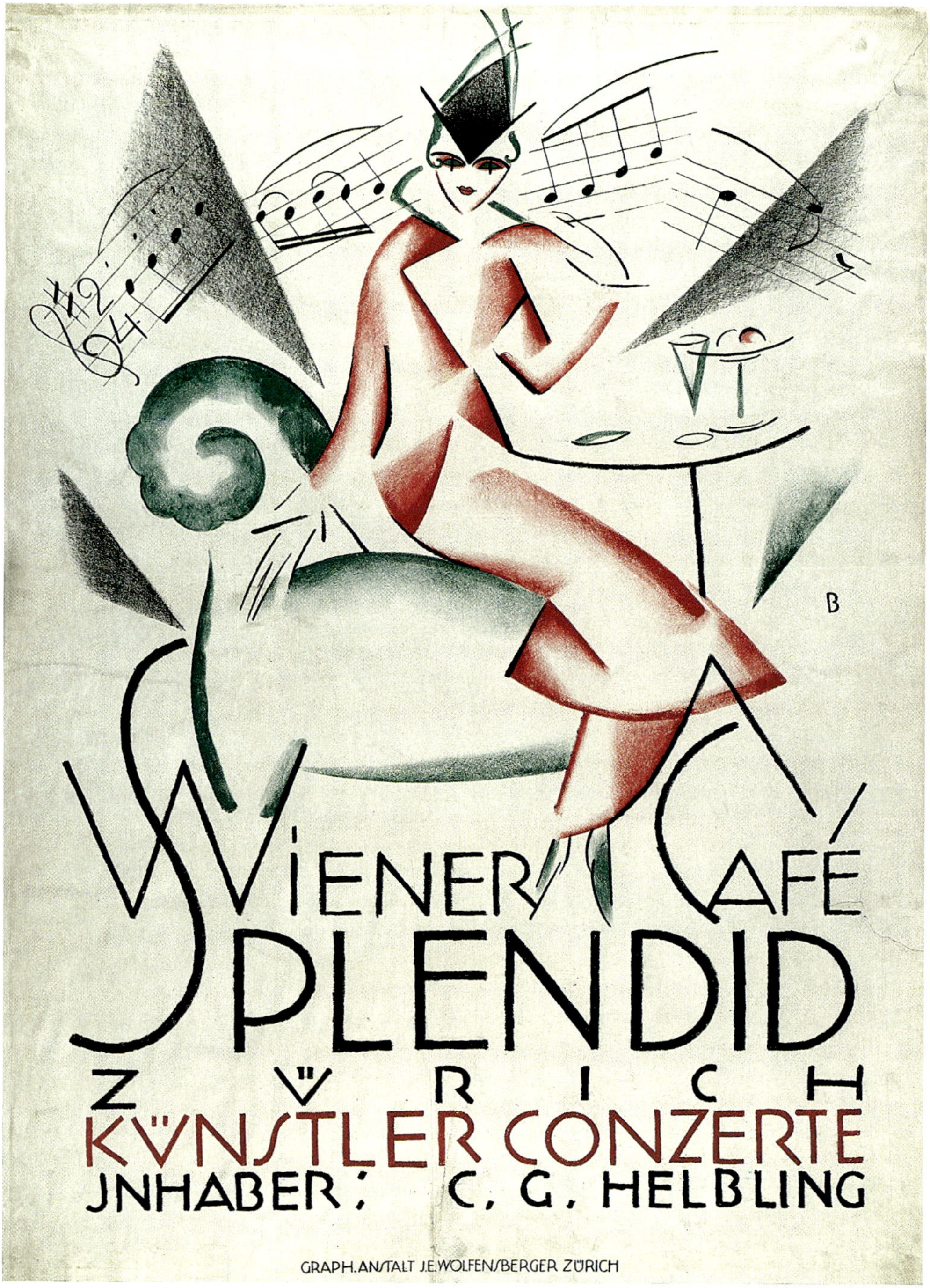

60 **Wiener Café Splendid Zürich / Künstler Conzerte**
Artiste concerts
1915

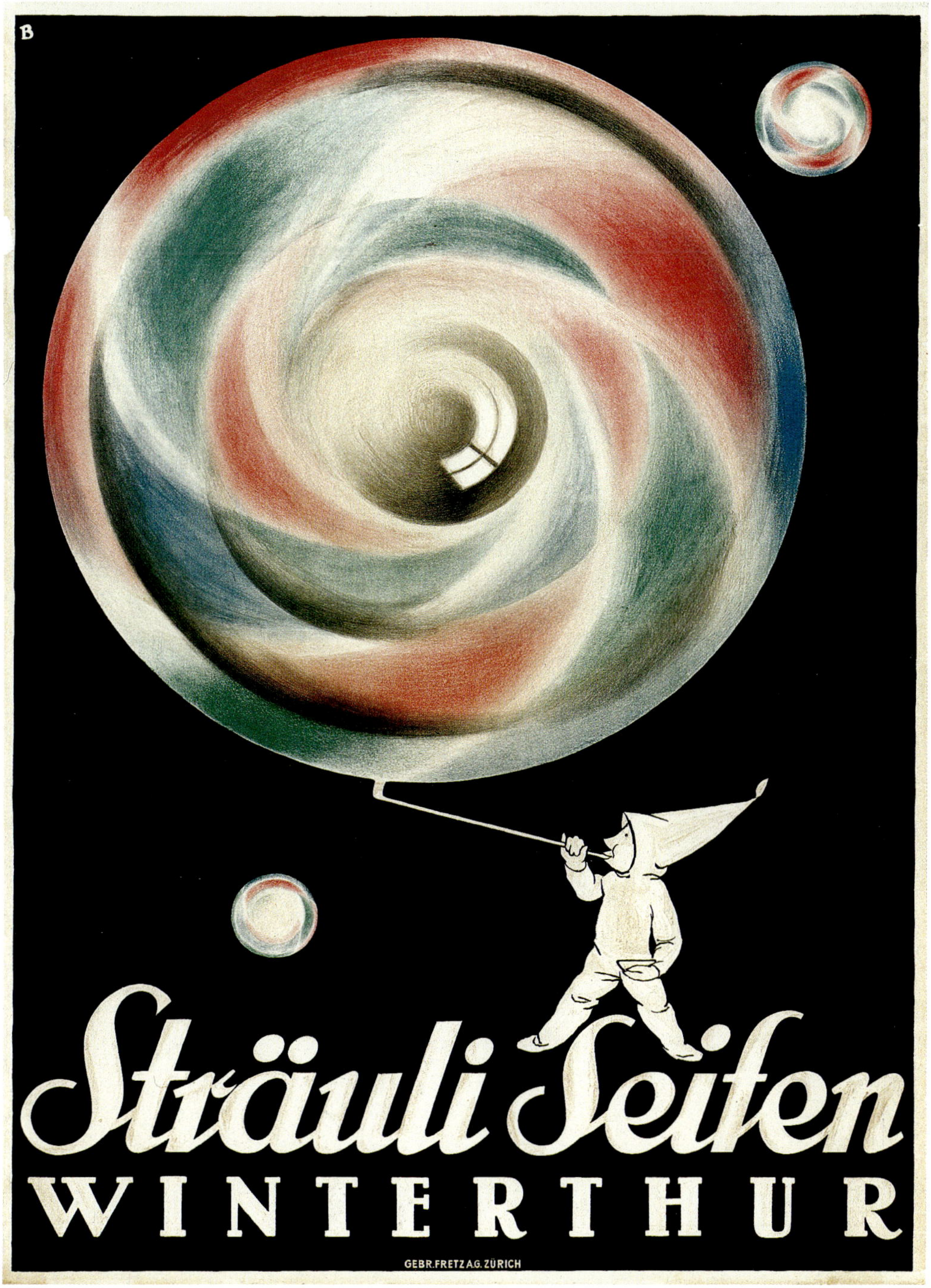

61 **Sträuli Seifen Winterthur**
Sträuli soaps, Winterthur
1925

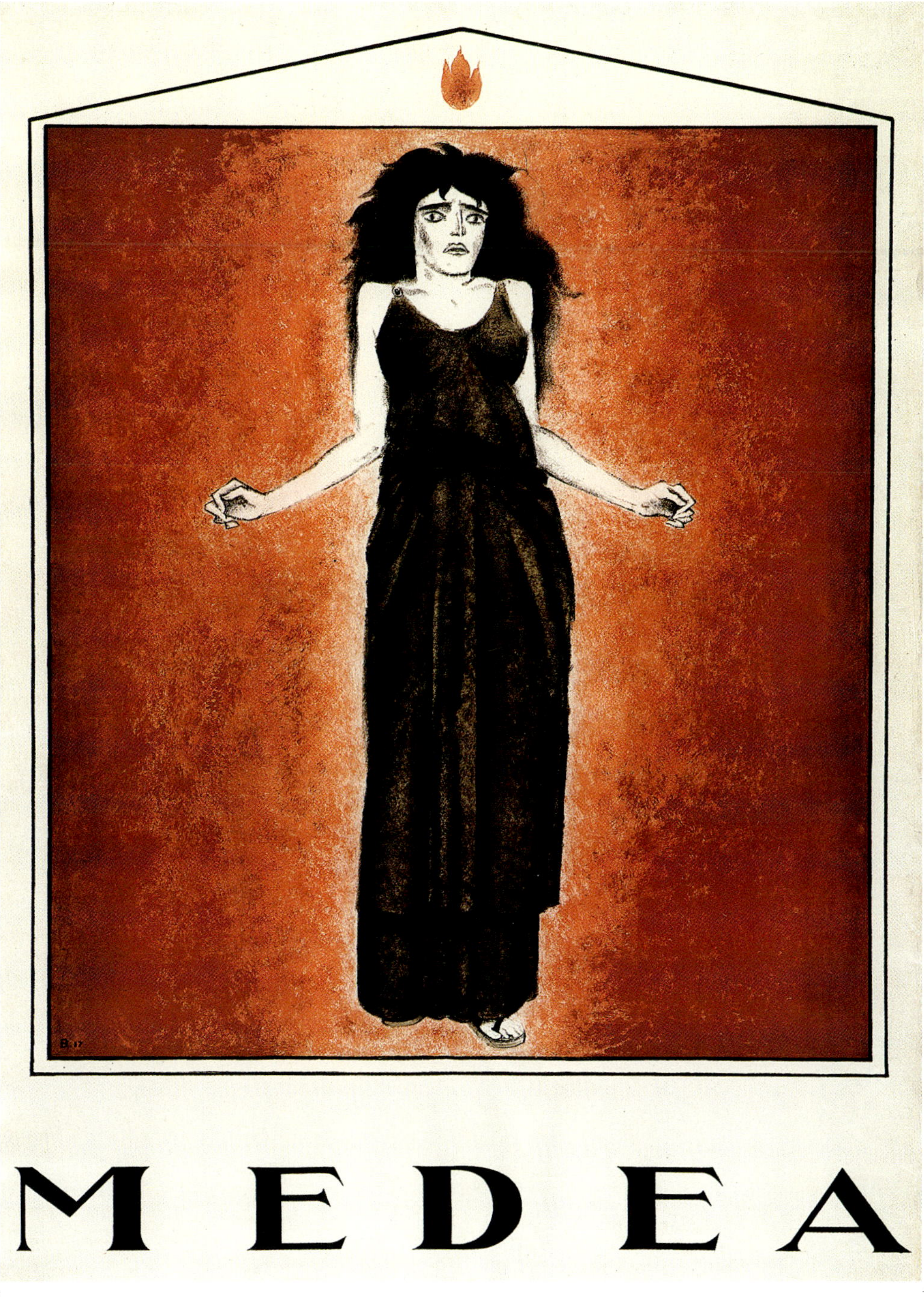

62 **Medea**
1917

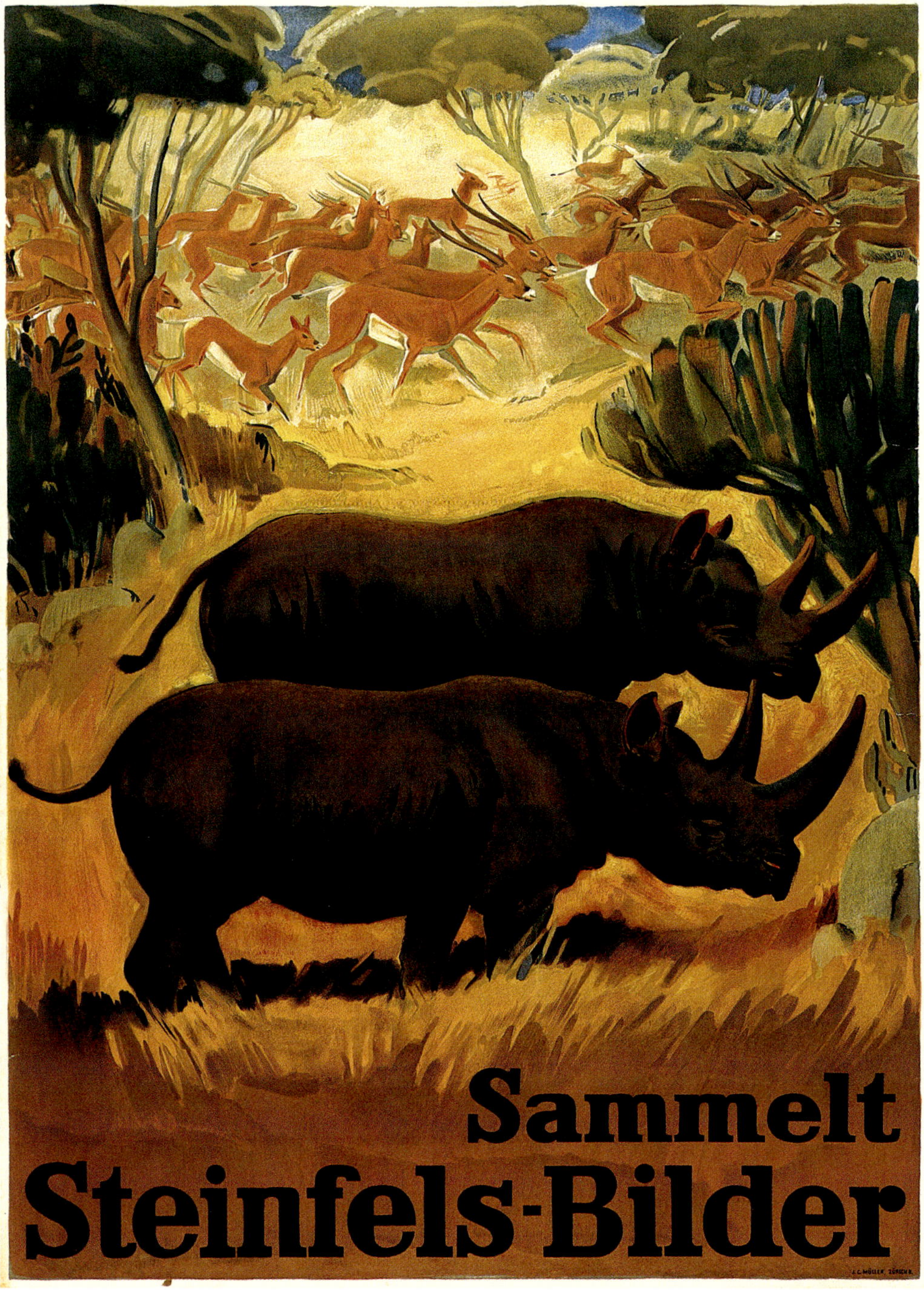

63 **Sammelt Steinfels-Bilder**
Collect Steinfels pictures
1934

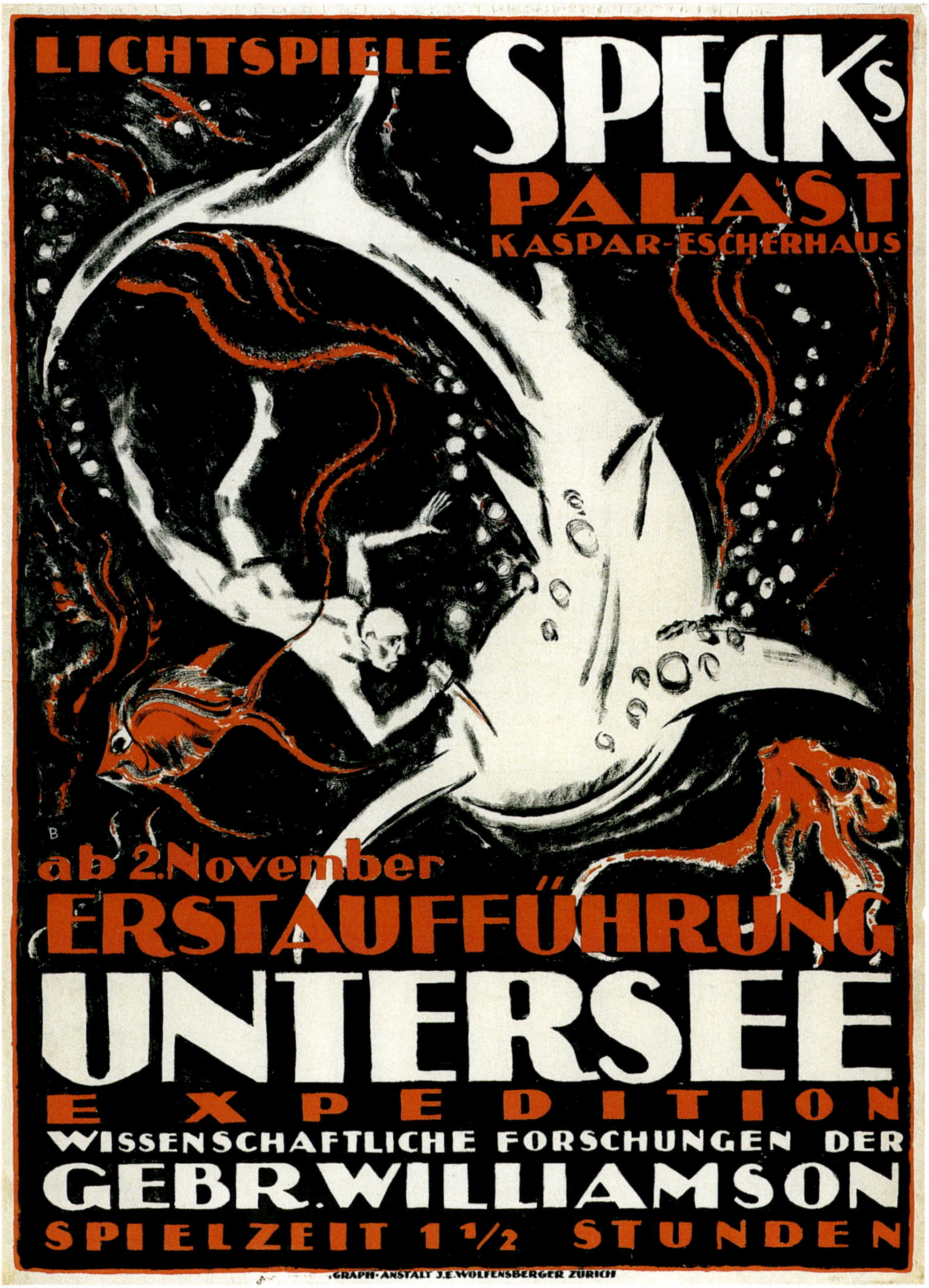

64 **Lichtspiele Speck's Palast**
Speck's Palast cinema
1916

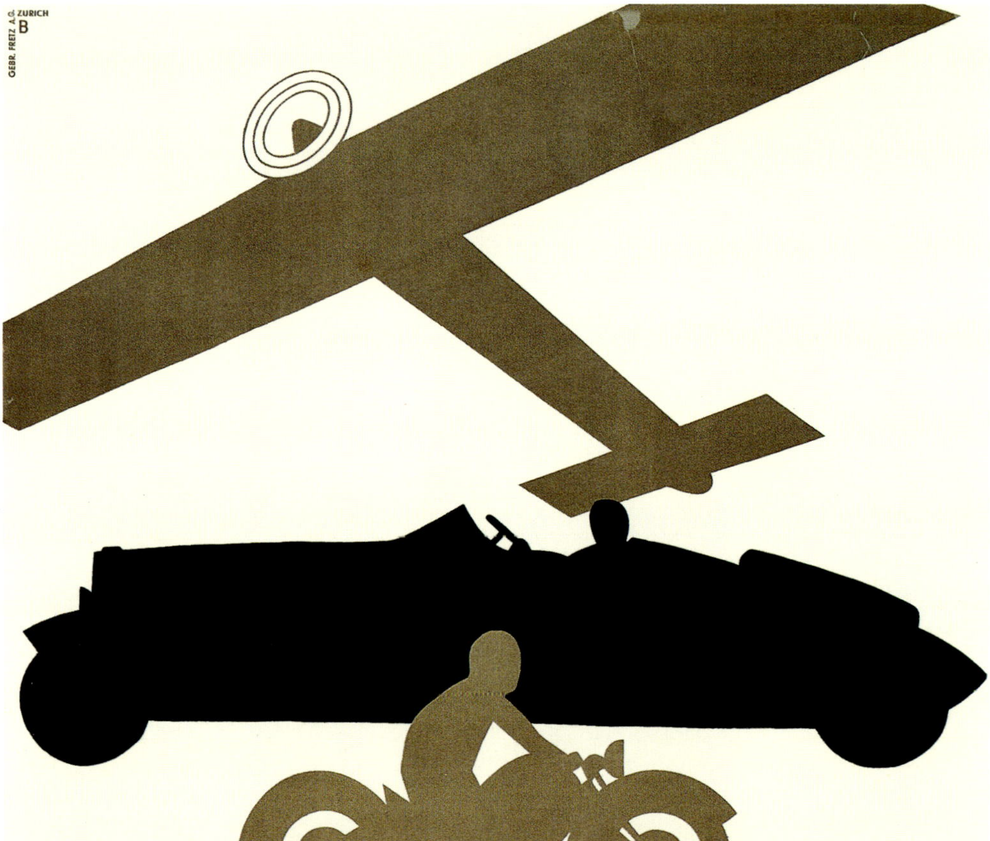

65 **Motor Comptoir Zürich 1932**
1932

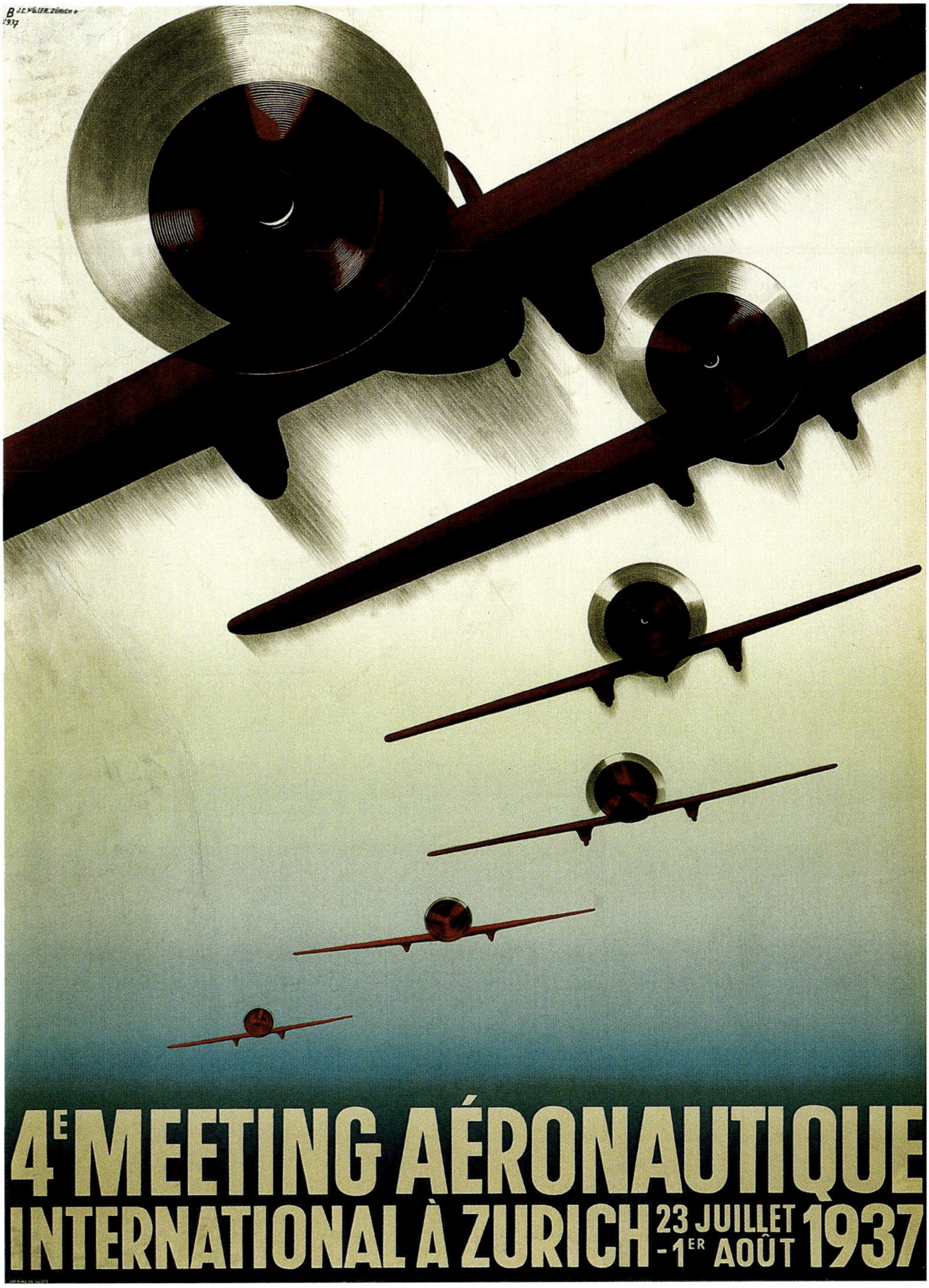

66 **IV. Internationales Flugmeeting Zürich**
4th Zurich International Air Show
1937

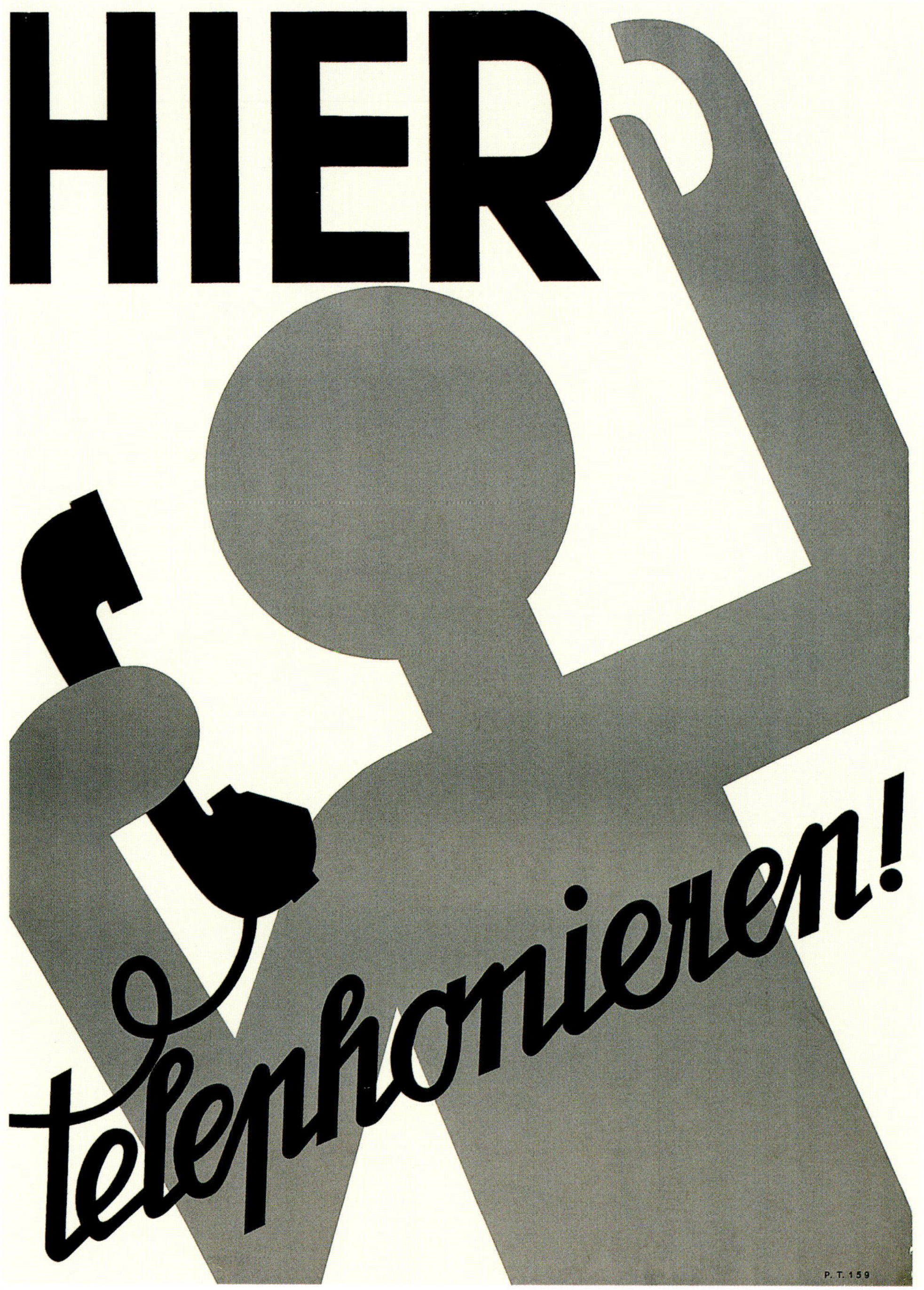

67 **Hier telephonieren!**
Telephone here!
1933

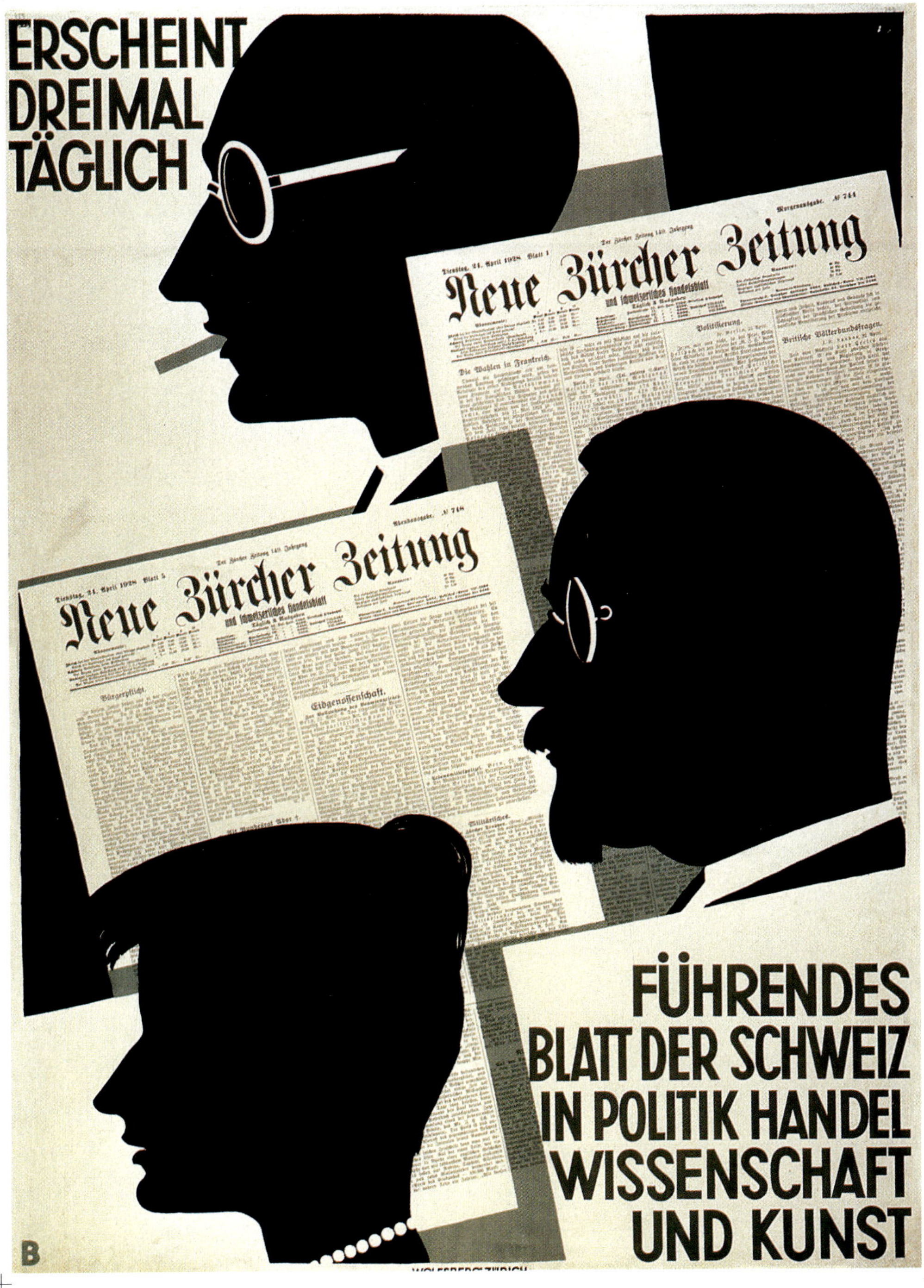

68 ***Neue Zürcher Zeitung***
1928

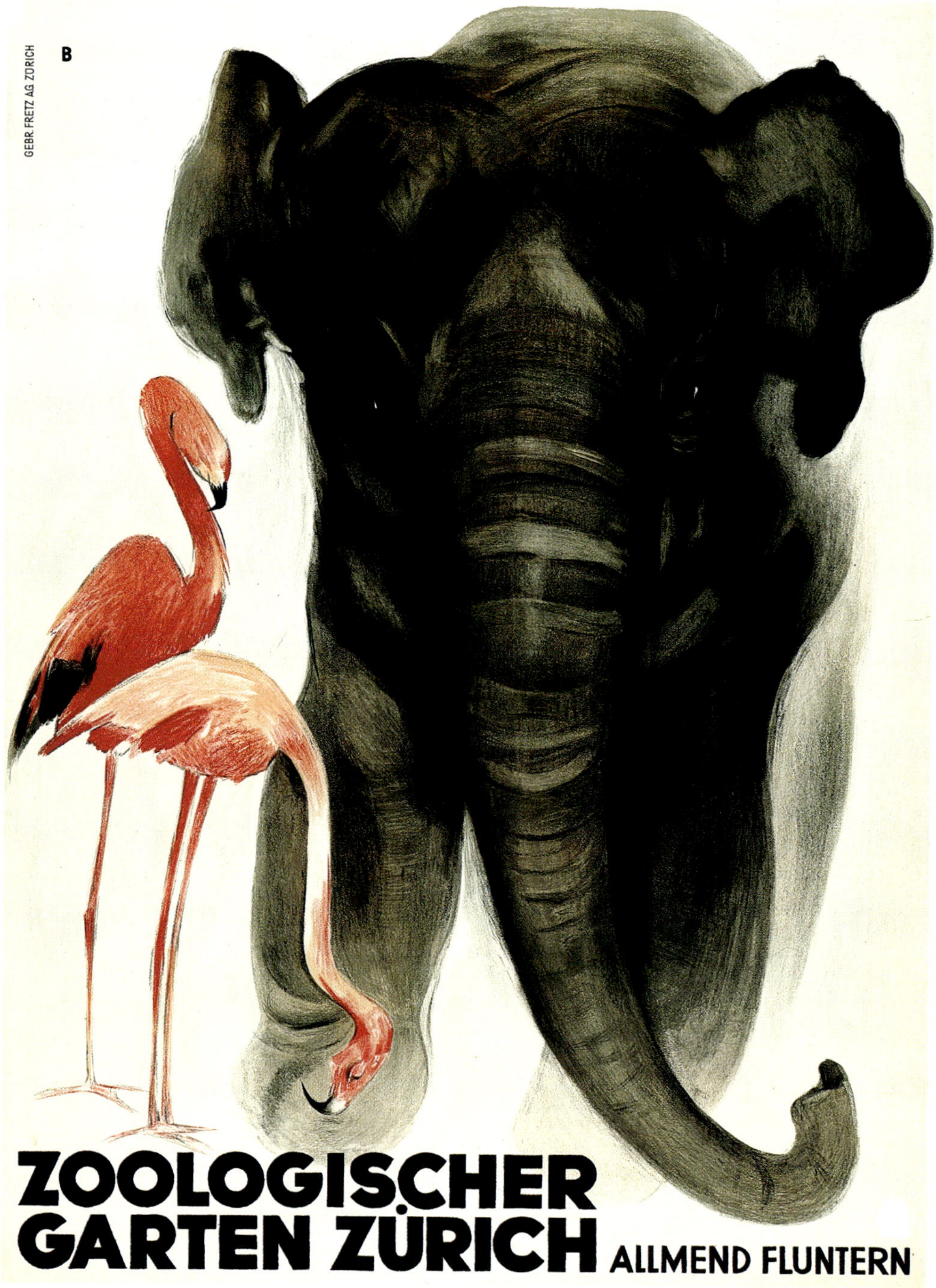

69 **Zoologischer Garten Zürich**
Zurich Zoological Gardens
1929

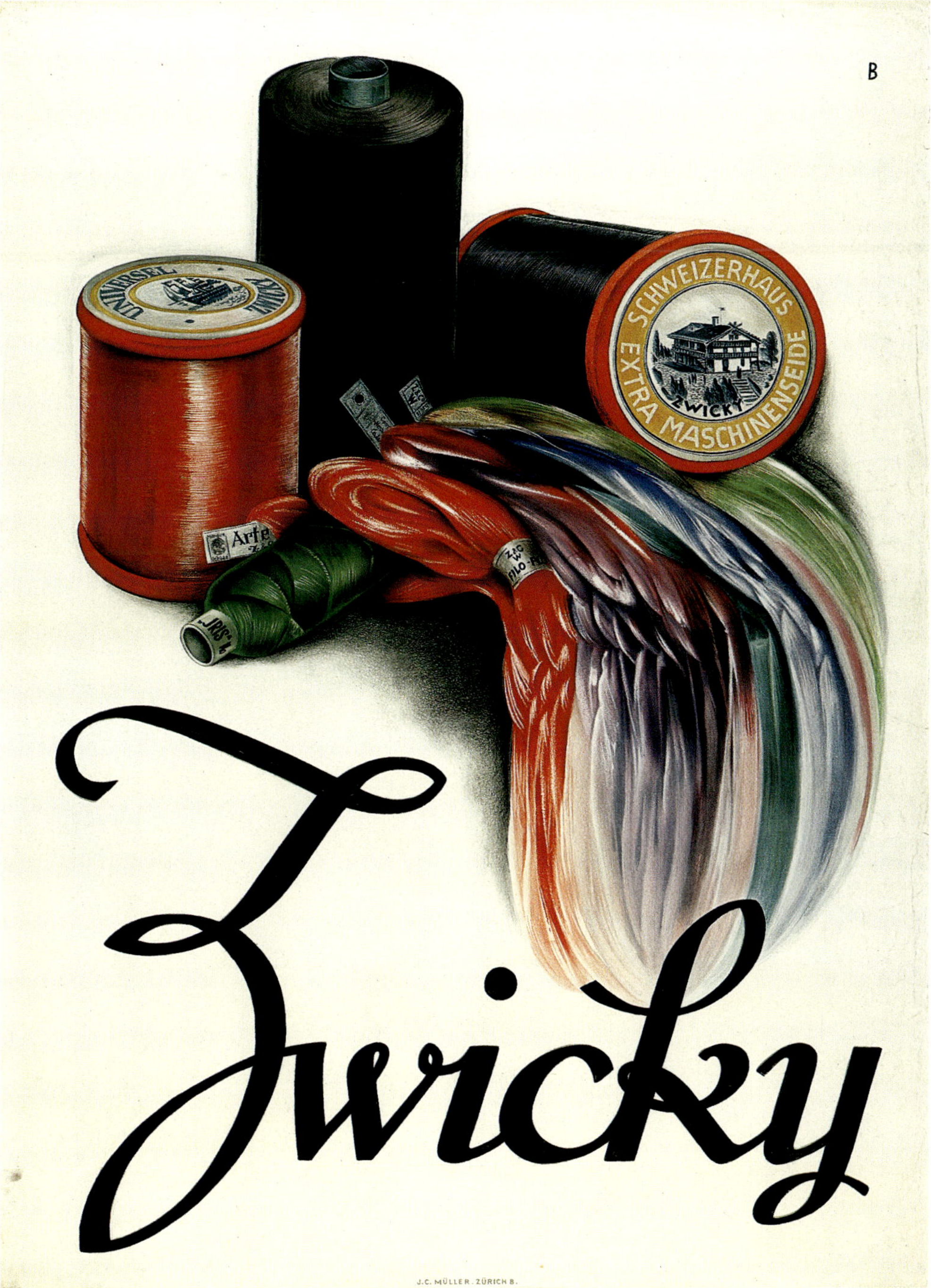

70 **Zwicky Näh- & Stickseide**
Zwicky sewing and embroidery silk
1927

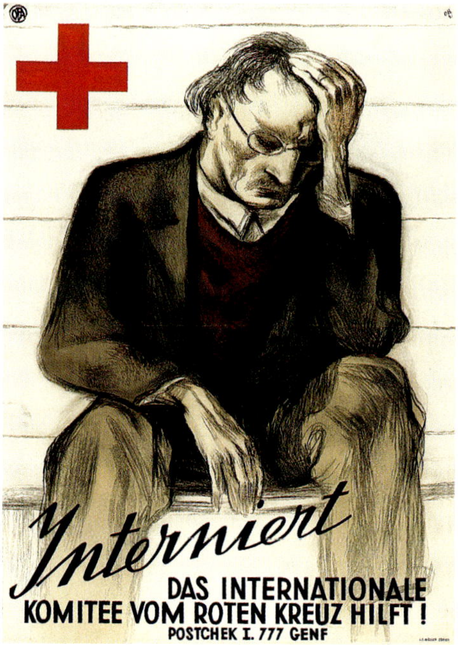

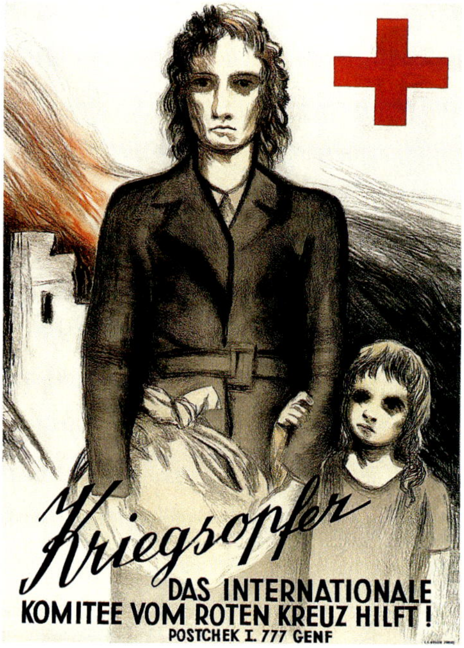

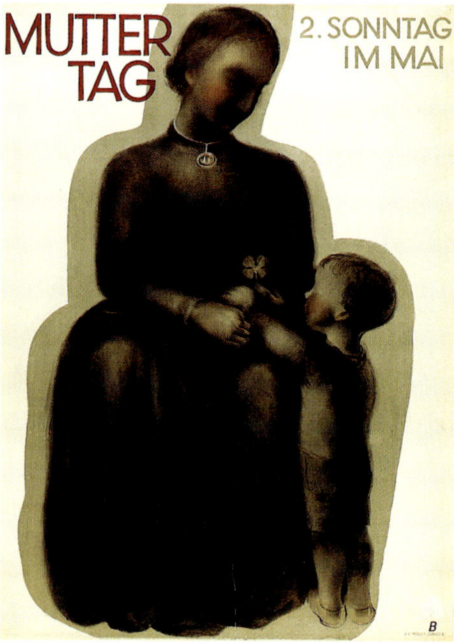

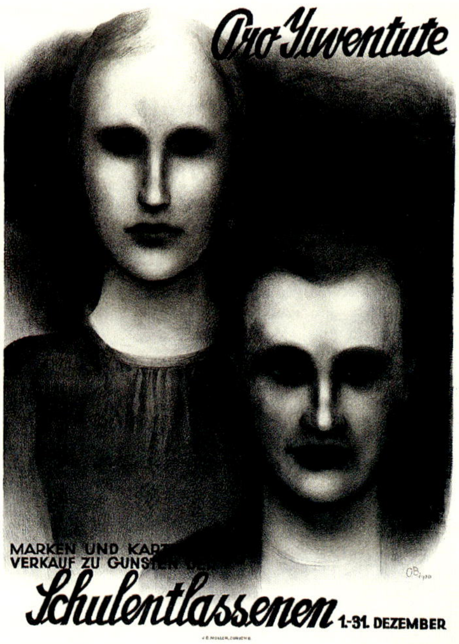

71 **Interniert / Das Internationale Komitee vom Roten Kreuz hilft! – Interned / The International Red Cross Committee helps!** 1943

72 **Muttertag – Mother's Day** 1932

73 **Kriegsopfer / Das Internationale Komitee vom Roten Kreuz hilft! – War victims / The International Red Cross Committee helps!** 1943

74 **Pro Juventute / Marken und Kartenverkauf zu Gunsten der Schulentlassenen – Pro Juventute / Stamp and ticket sales to benefit graduates** 1930

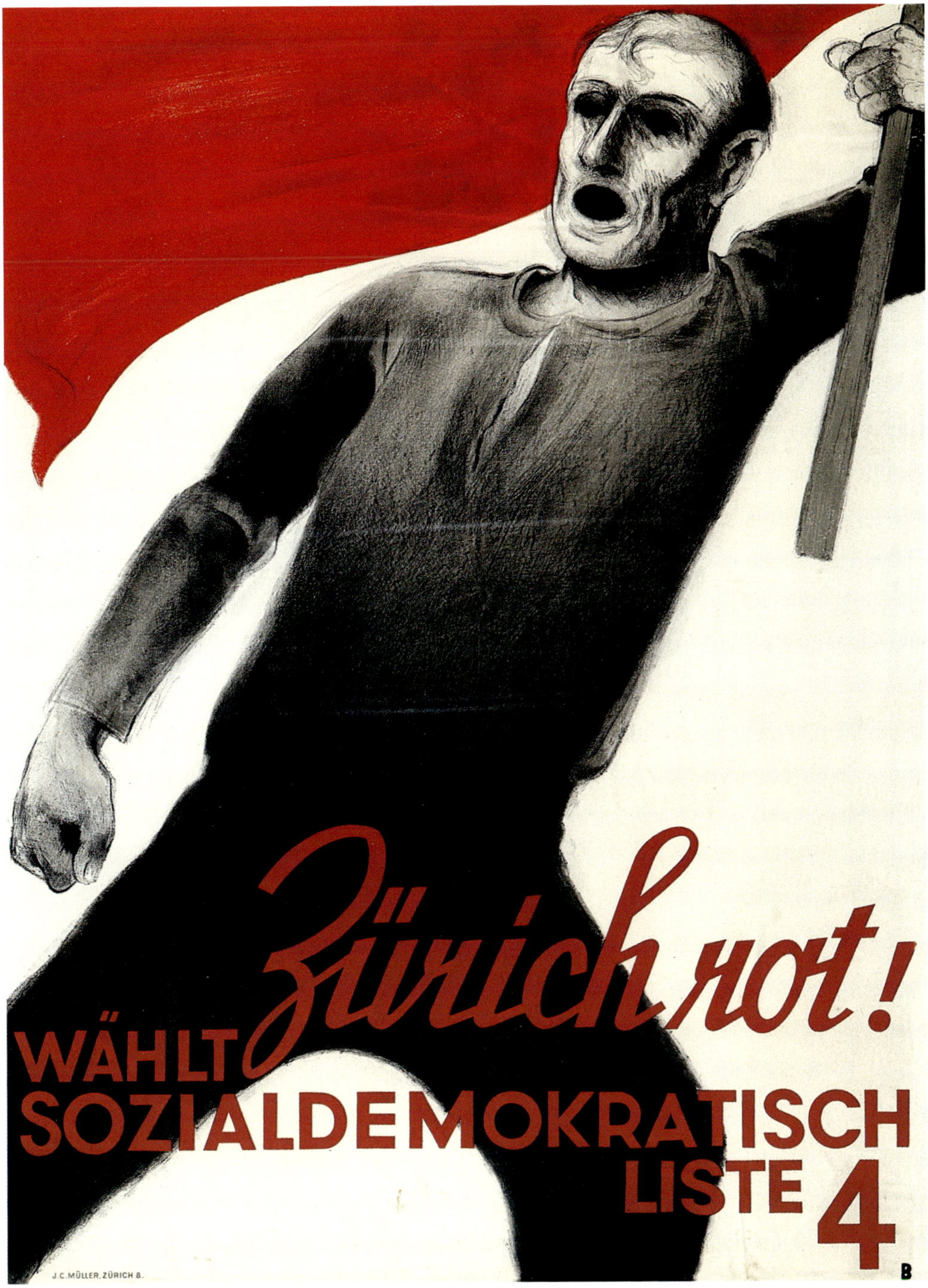

75 **Zürich rot! Wählt sozialdemokratisch / Liste 4**
Red Zurich! Vote Social Democrat / List 4
1931

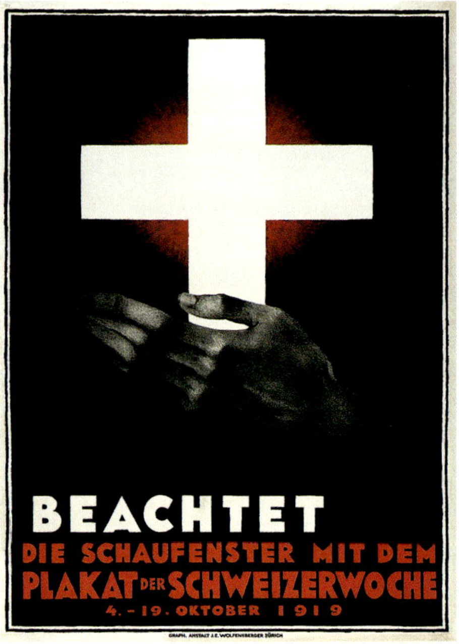

76 **Beachtet die Schaufenster mit dem Plakat der Schweizerwoche – Watch for the shop windows with the "Swiss Week" poster** 1919

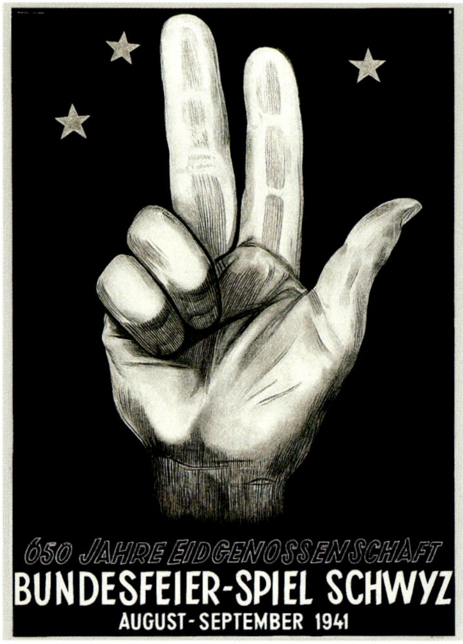

78 **Bundesfeier-Spiel Schwyz**
Schwyz Federal Celebration Games
1941

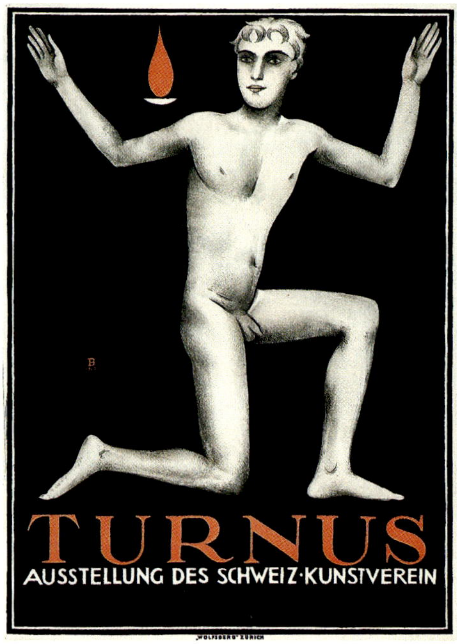

77 **Turnus / Ausstellung des Schweiz. Kunstverein**
Exhibition by the Swiss Art Association
1919

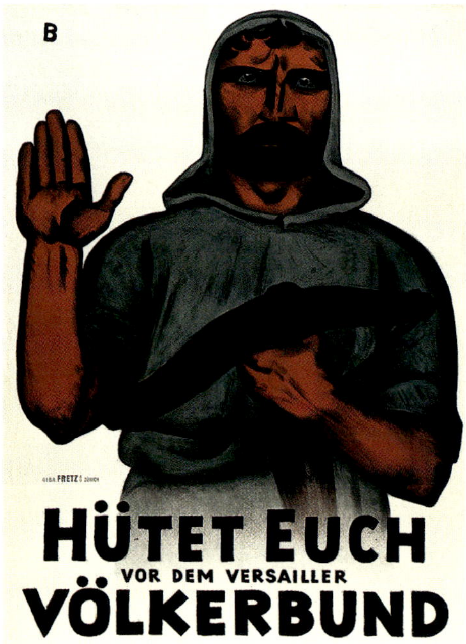

79 **Hütet euch vor dem Versailler Völkerbund**
Beware of the Versailles League of Nations
1920

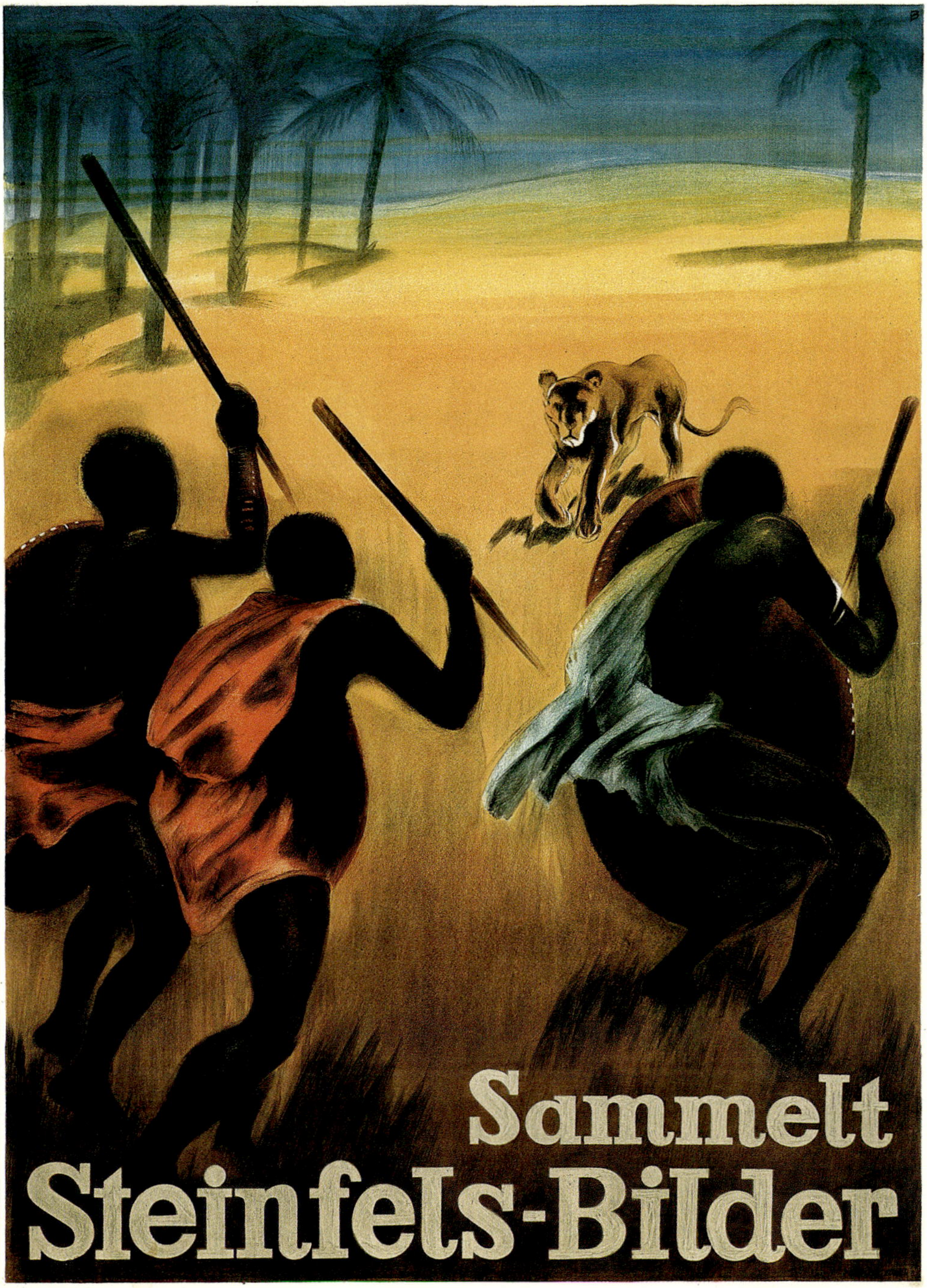

80 **Sammelt Steinfels-Bilder**
Collect Steinfels pictures
1934

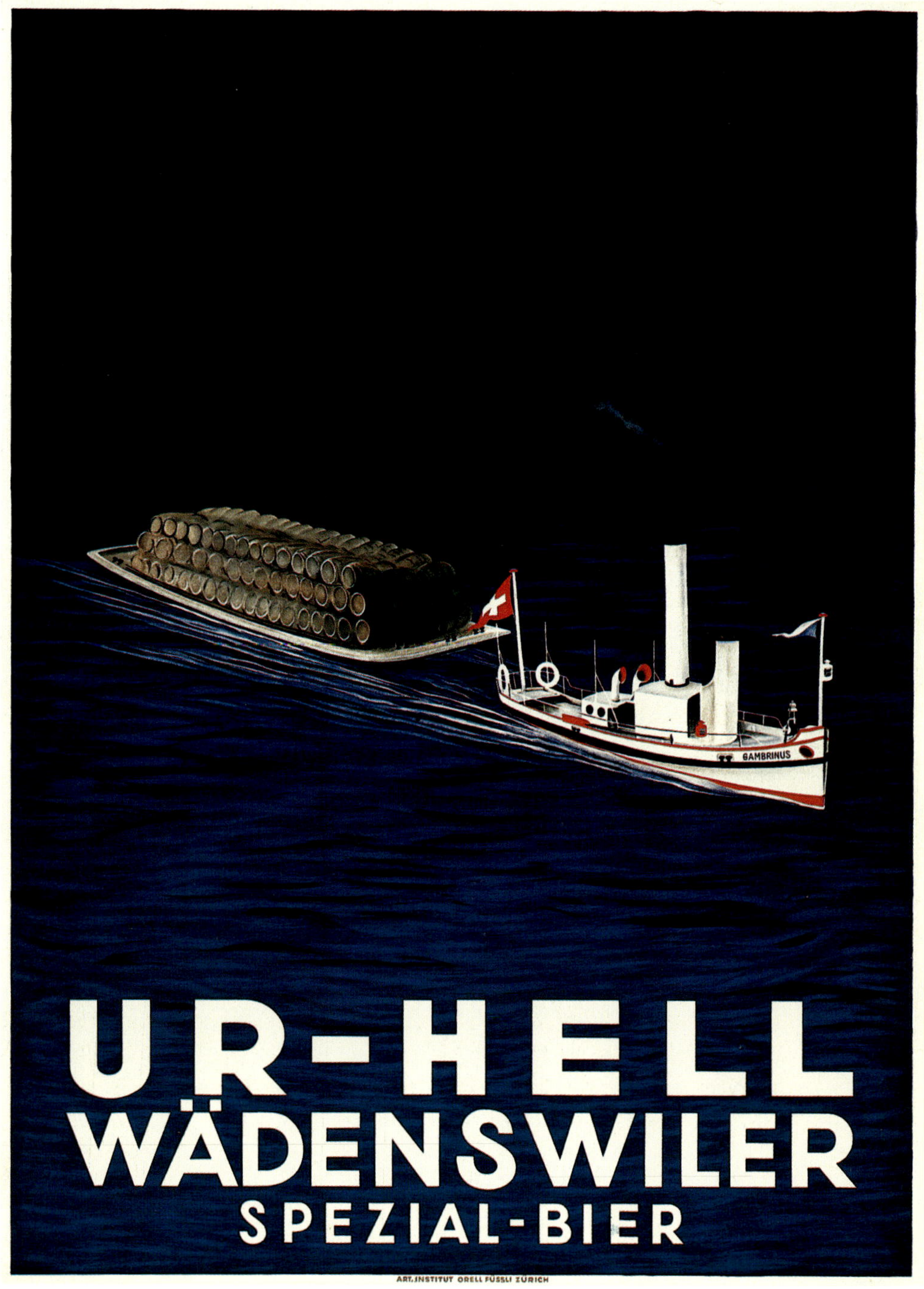

81 **Ur-Hell / Wädenswiler Spezial-Bier**
Premium light / Wädenswiler special beer
ca. 1925

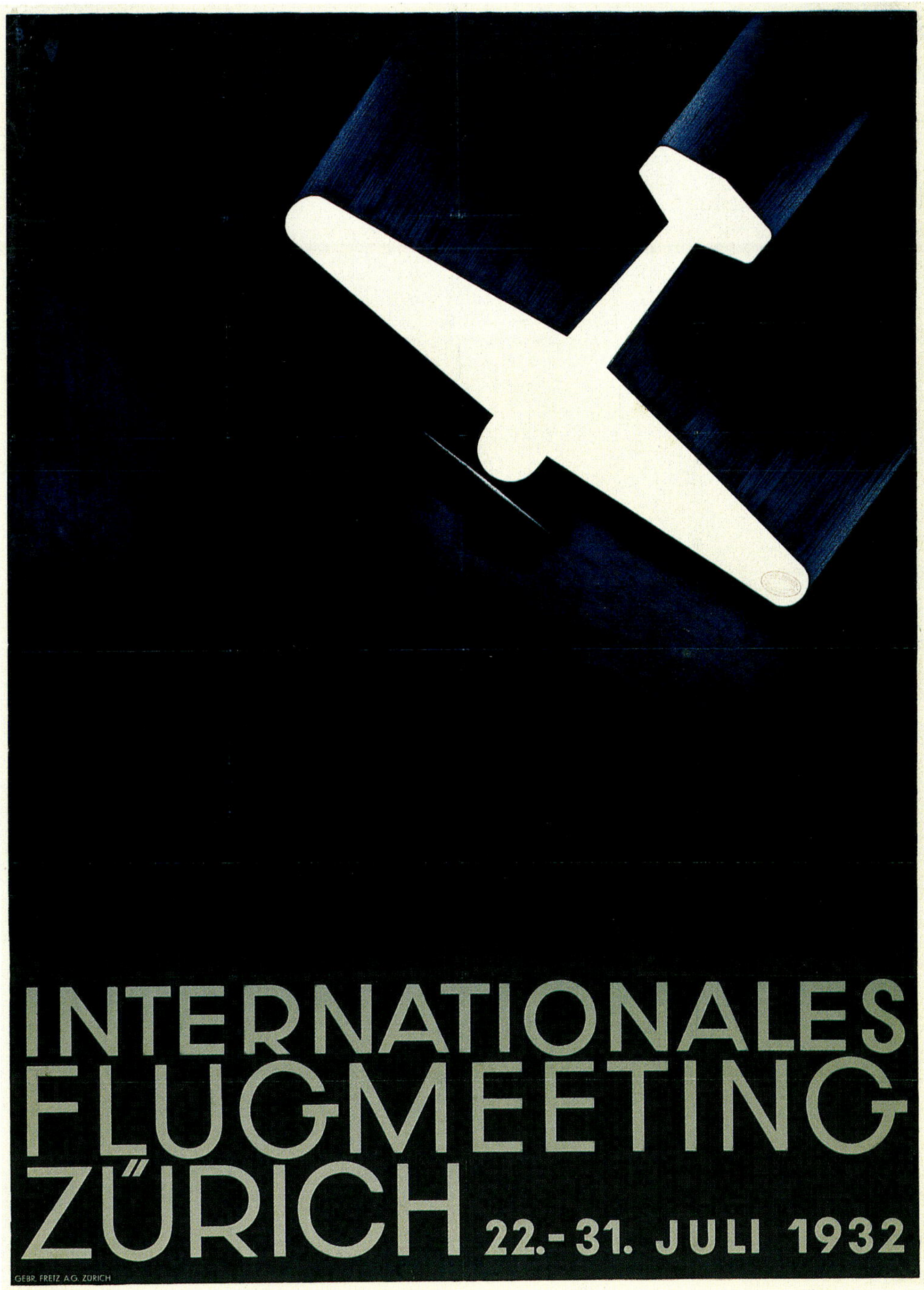

82 **Internationales Flugmeeting Zürich**
Zurich International Air Show
1932

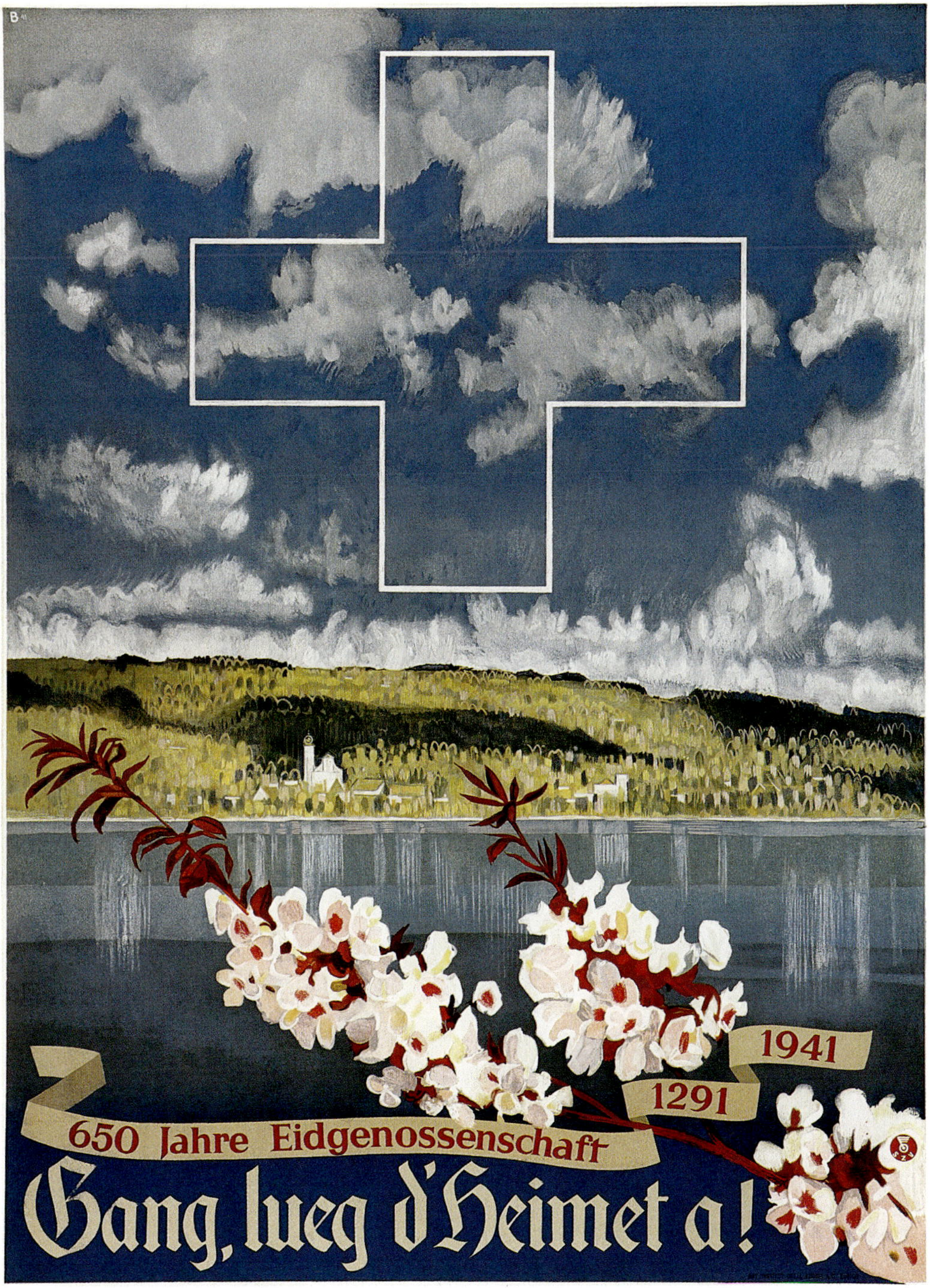

83 **Gang, lueg d'Heimet a!**
Go visit your homeland!
1941

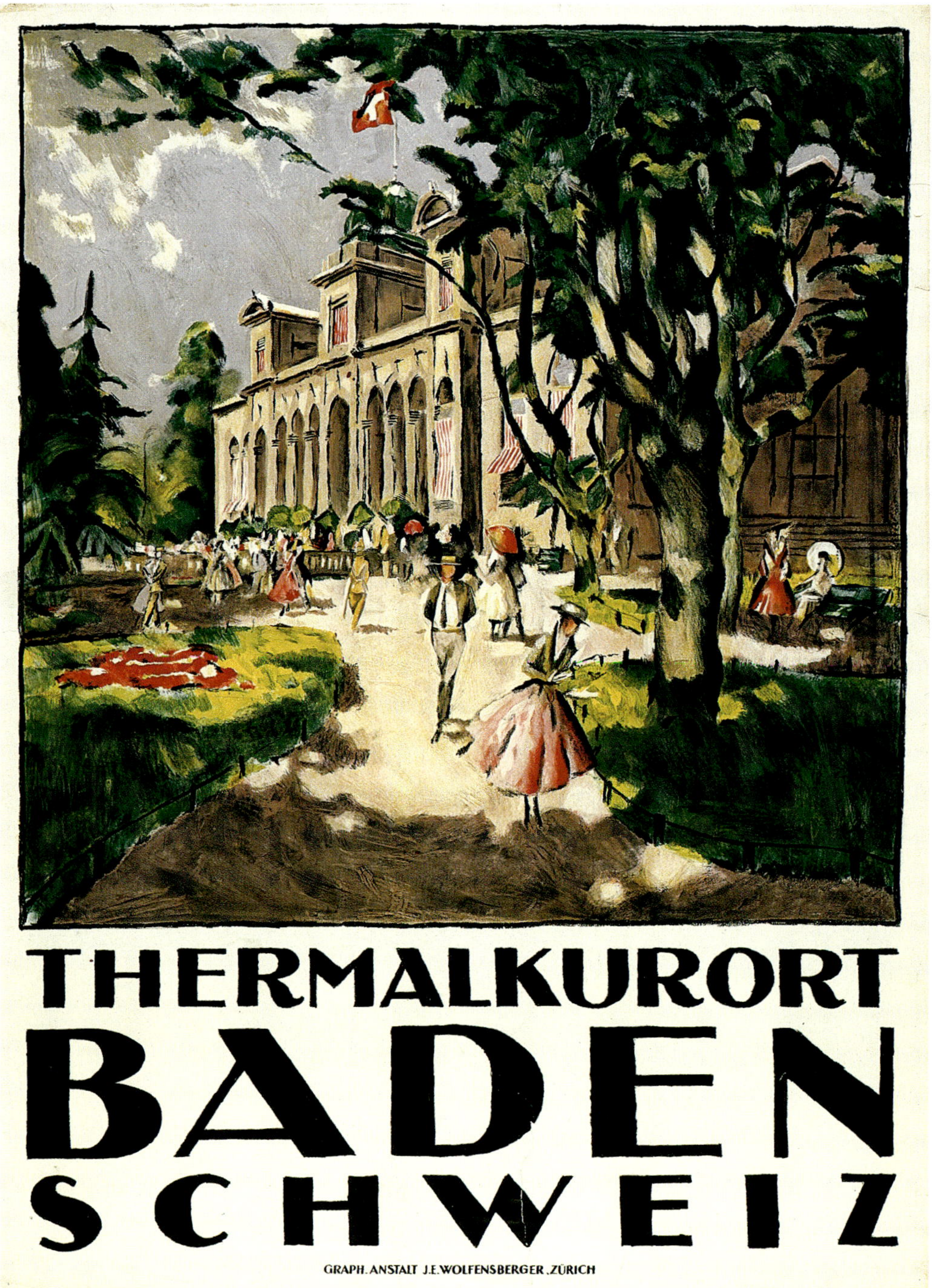

84 **Thermalkurort Baden Schweiz**
Thermal spa, Baden, Switzerland
1916

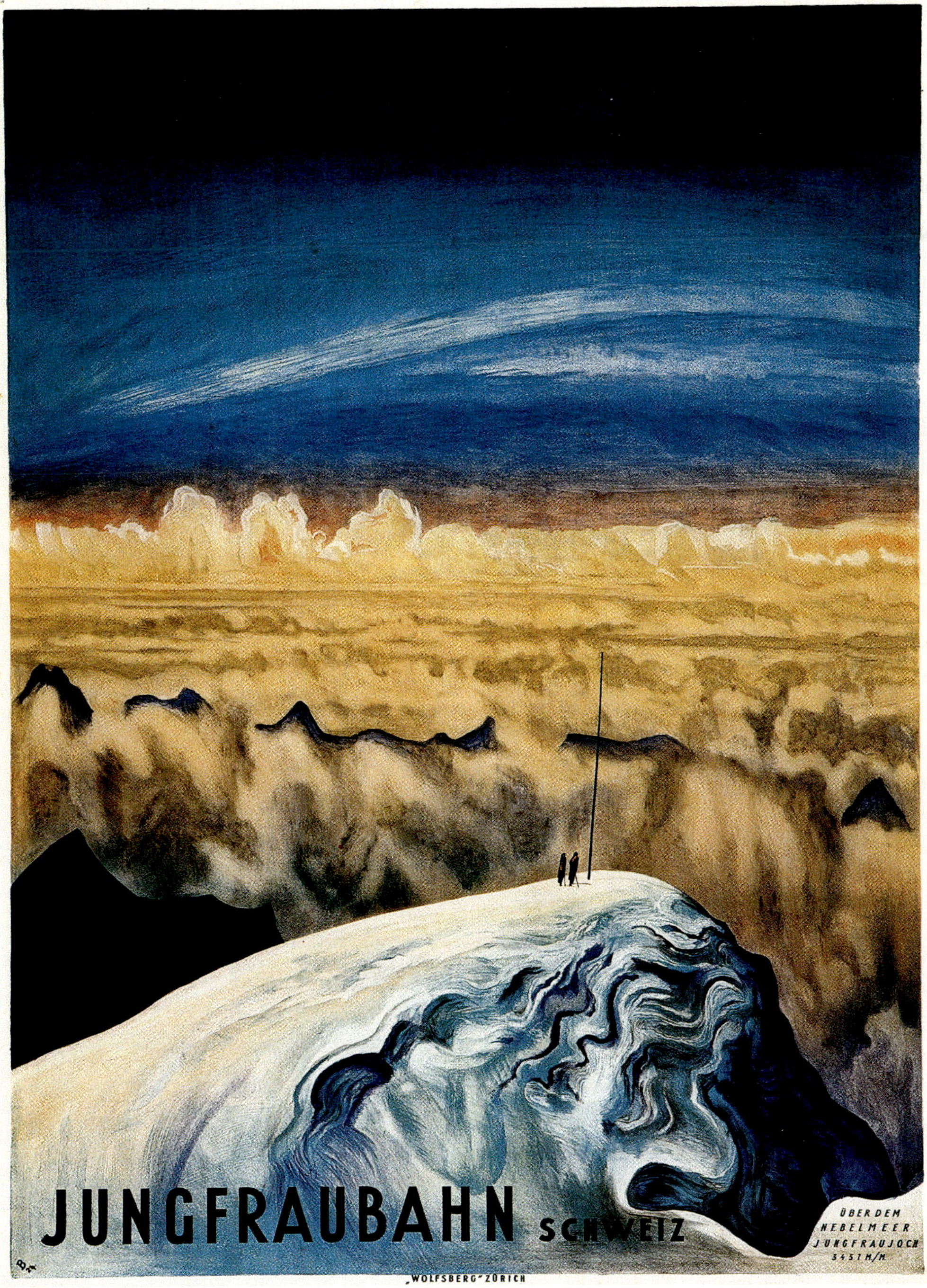

85 **Jungfraubahn Schweiz**
Jungfrau railway, Switzerland
1924

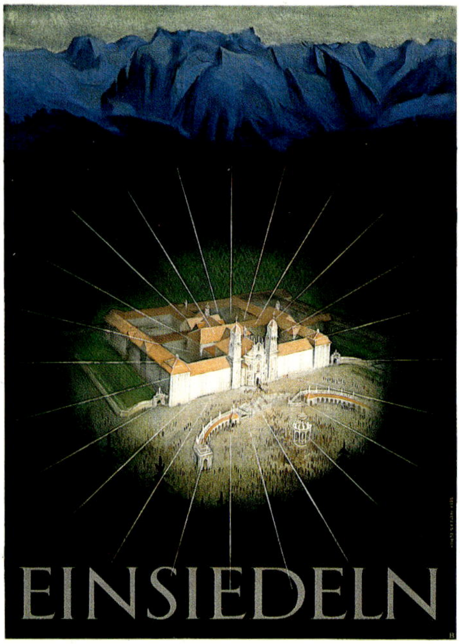

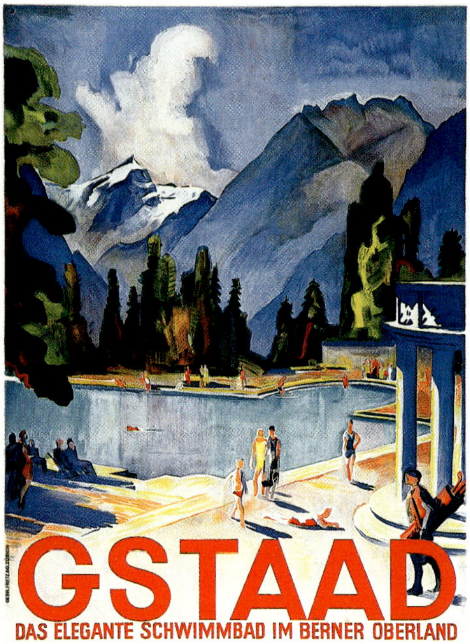

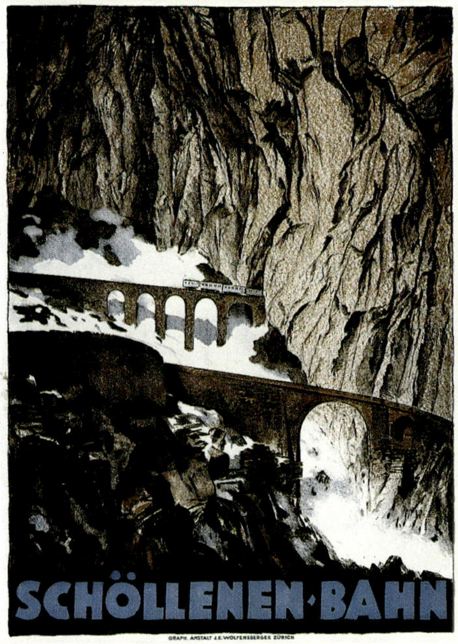

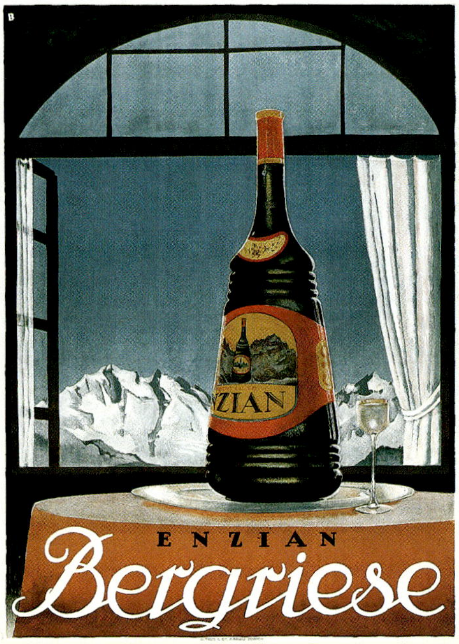

86 **Einsiedeln**
1934

87 **Schöllenen-Bahn**
Schöllenen railway
1919

88 **Gstaad / Das elegante Schwimmbad im Berner Oberland – The elegant swimming pool in the Bernese Oberland**
1929

89 **Enzian Bergriese**
1923

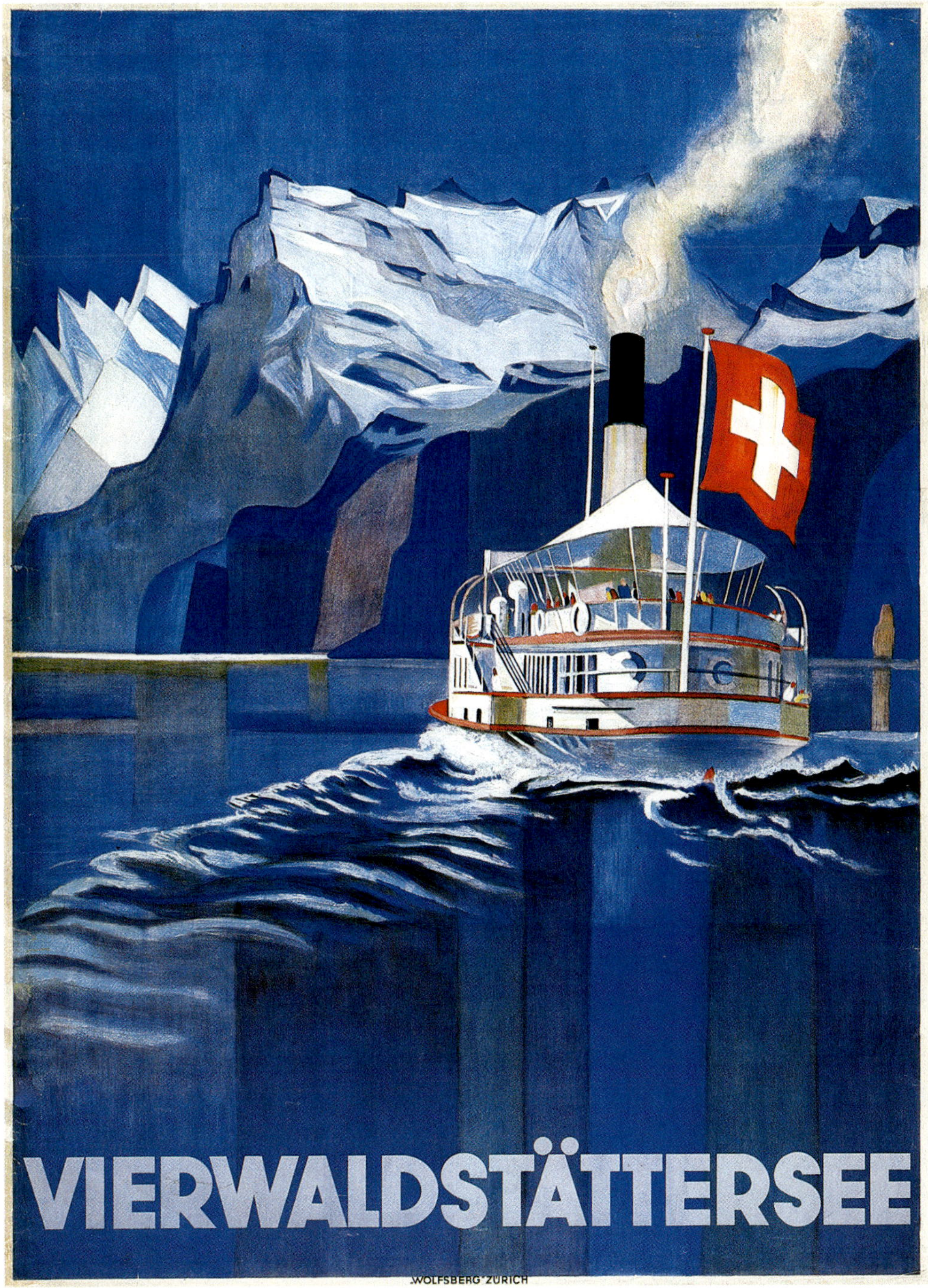

90 **Vierwaldstättersee**
Lake Lucerne
1928

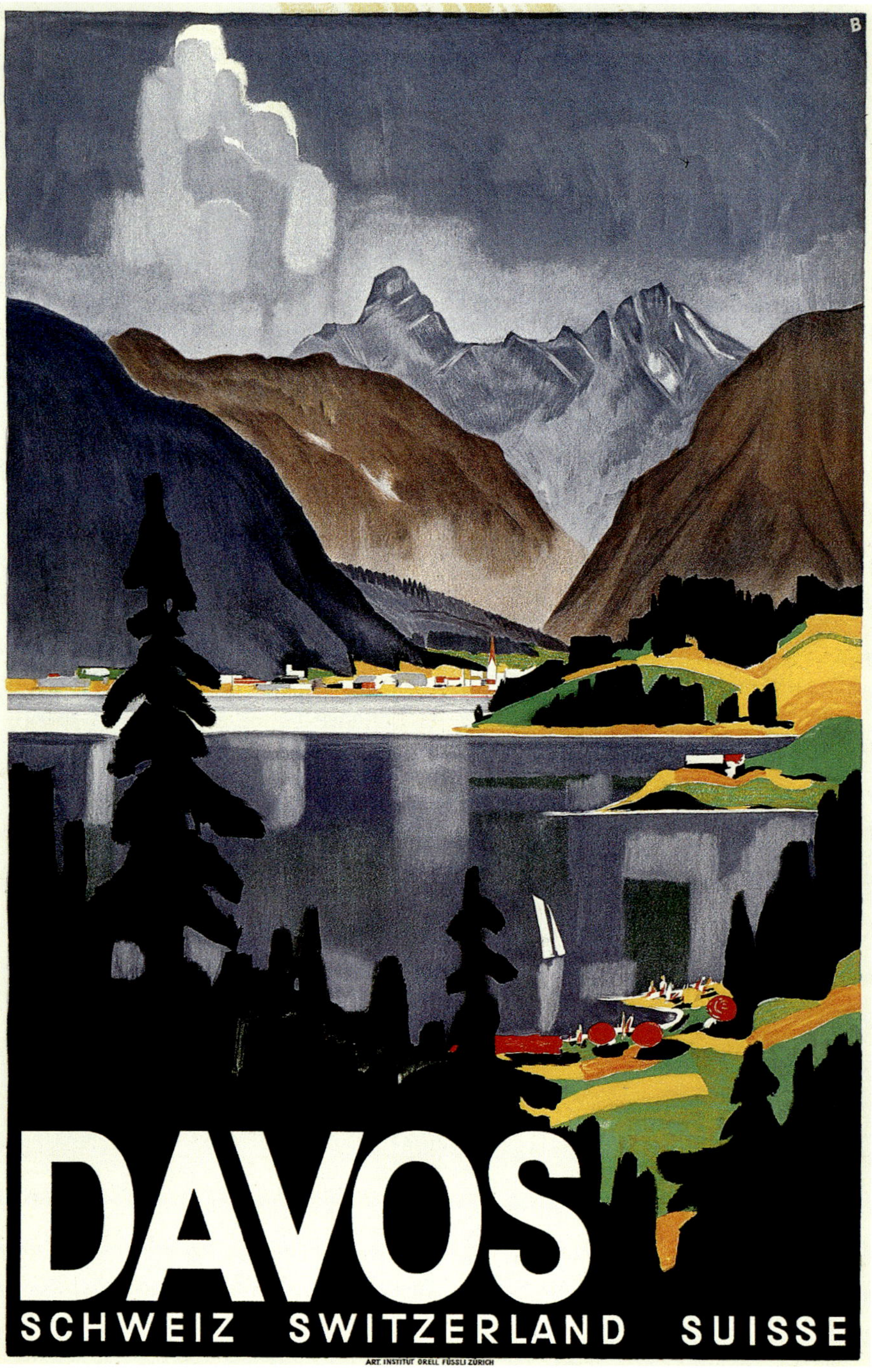

91 **Davos / Schweiz / Switzerland / Suisse**
1932

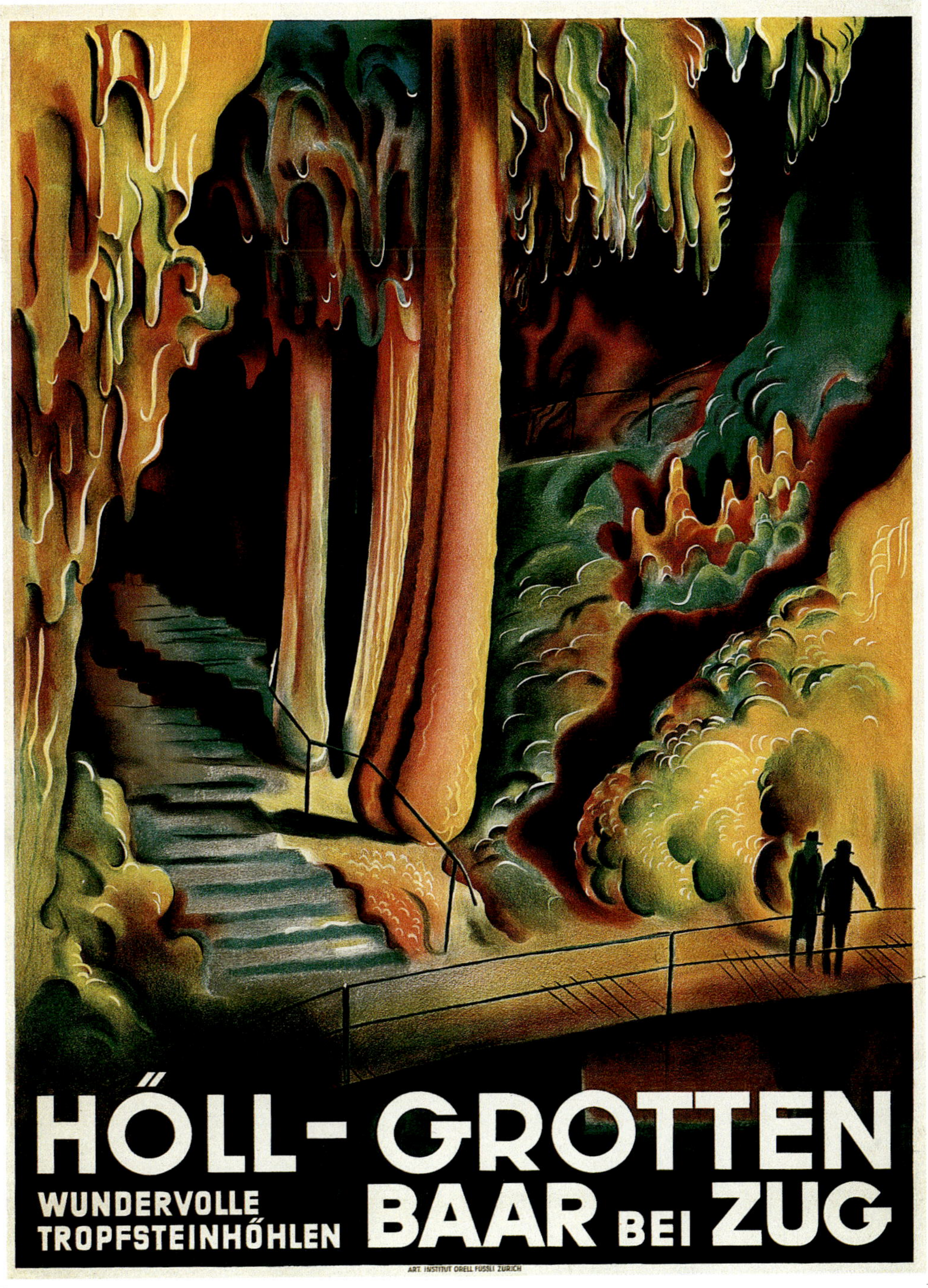

92 **Höll-Grotten / Baar bei Zug**
Höll Grottoes / Baar near Zug
ca. 1931

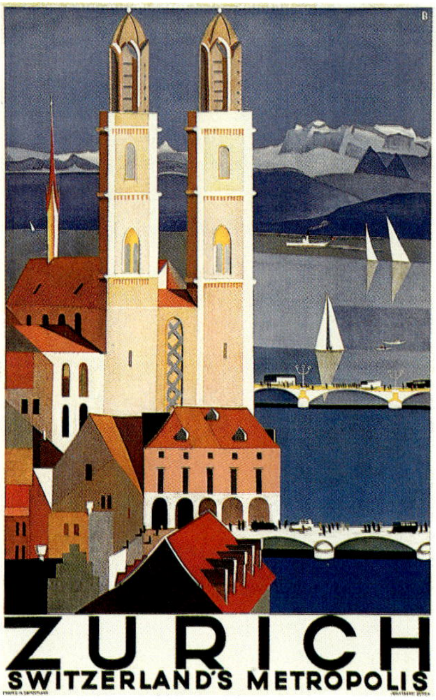

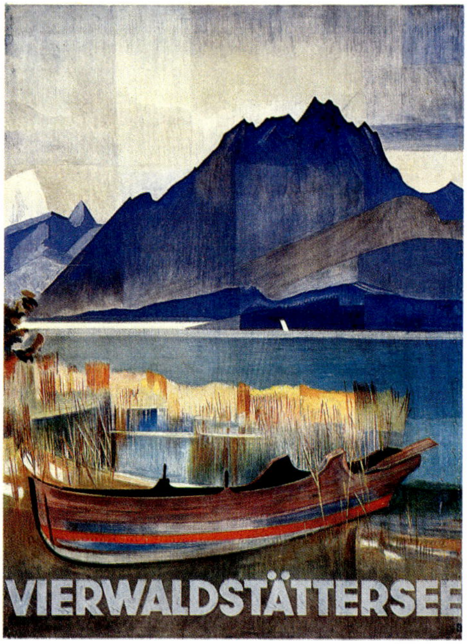

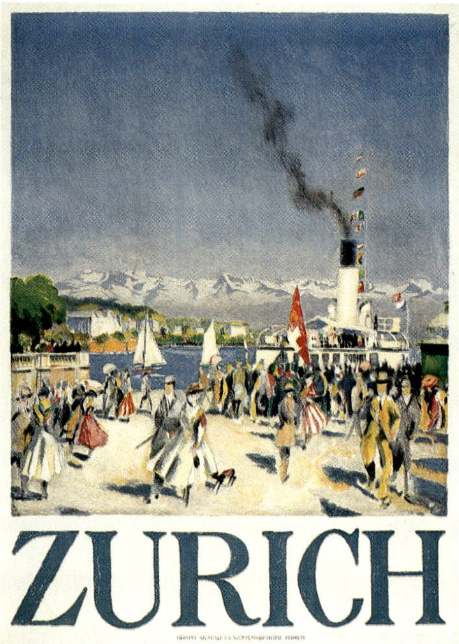

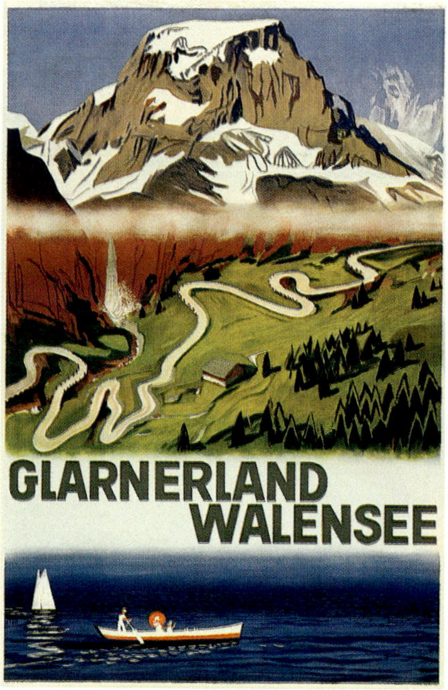

93 **Zurich / Switzerland's Metropolis**
Zürich / Die Metropole der Schweiz
1929

94 **Zurich**
1916

95 **Vierwaldstättersee**
Lake Lucerne
1928

96 **Glarnerland / Walensee**
1944

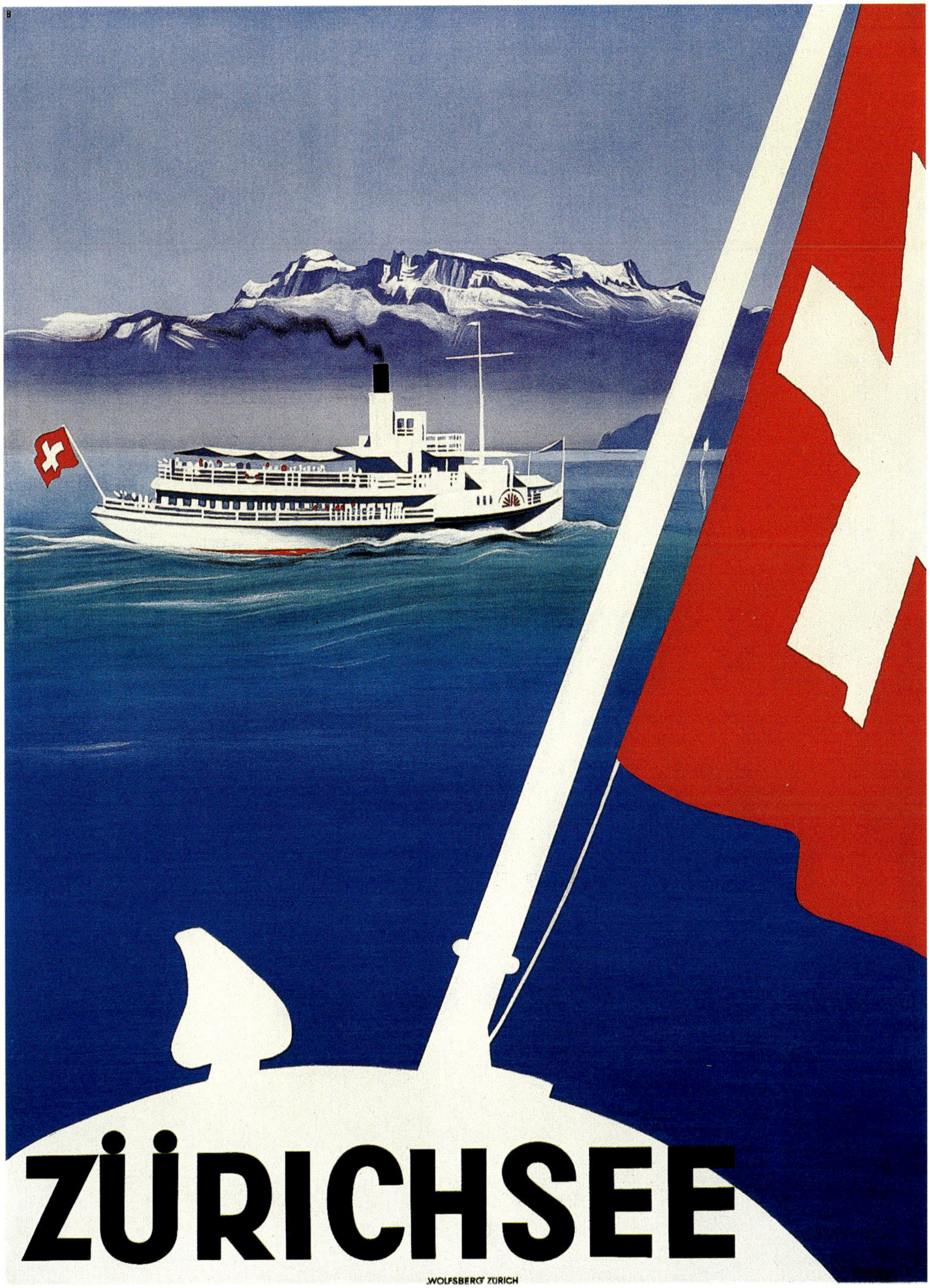

97 **Zürichsee**
Lake Zurich
1935

Biografie Otto Baumberger

1889
Otto Baumberger wird am 21. Mai 1889 in Altstetten, Zürich geboren. Nach Abbruch einer Textilzeichnerlehre Ausbildung zum Lithografen im Grafischen Atelier Emil Winter in Zürich. Während der Lehrzeit Besuch der Kunstgewerbeschule und der privaten Stadler-Schule. Der auch als Plakatgestalter bekannt gewordene Eduard Stiefel ist sein bevorzugter Lehrer.

1908
Während drei Jahren Studienaufenthalte in München, Berlin, Paris und London: Baumberger besucht Kurse an verschiedenen Kunstschulen und Akademien. Freundschaftliche Kontakte unter anderem mit Hermann Huber, Reinhold Kündig und Hugo Laubi.

1910
Erste Teilnahme an einer Ausstellung (Zürcher Kunstgesellschaft) mit Zeichnungen der Pariser Banlieue. In der Folge bis in die 1950er Jahre regelmässige Präsenz bei zahlreichen Schweizer Gruppenausstellungen.

1911
Anstellung als Lithograf in der Graphischen Anstalt J.E. Wolfensberger, Zürich. Als Reproduktionslithograf macht Baumberger Bekanntschaft mit zahlreichen Künstlern seiner Zeit.

1913
Baumberger reist erneut nach Paris und ermöglicht sich einen längeren Aufenthalt durch Plakatarbeiten für Wolfensberger. In Malerei und Grafik Auseinandersetzung mit Expressionismus und Kubismus. Erst der Kriegsausbruch zwingt zu Heimkehr und Grenzdienst. Noch während des Krieges: breite gebrauchsgrafische Tätigkeit.

1915
Heirat mit Hanni Manz; 1918 Geburt der Tochter Gertrud.

1917
Die deutsche Zeitschrift *Das Plakat* widmet Baumberger eine ausführlich kommentierte Werkübersicht.

1918
Familiäre Schwierigkeiten und Trennung. Für kurze Zeit als künstlerischer Leiter bei Wolfensberger, «verantwortlich für Entwurf und Druck», danach wieder im freien Auftragsverhältnis.

1920
Reise durch das verelendete Nachkriegsdeutschland nach Berlin. Kontakte zu Verlegern und Sammlern. Über eine Empfehlung an Max Reinhardt kommt ein Engagement als Bühnenbildner am Deutschen Theater zustande («Urfaust»). Eine Daueranstellung schlägt Baumberger aus.

1922
Zurück in Zürich; Antritt einer Hilfslehrerstelle an der Kunstgewerbeschule Zürich. Intensive Plakatproduktion. Immer breiteres Arbeitsfeld: Festschriften und Mappenwerke für Stadt und Kanton Zürich, Briefmarken für die PTT, Buchillustrationen, Wandmalereien. Baumberger ist überdies als Mitarbeiter beim *Nebelspalter* und am Zürcher Stadttheater tätig.

1927
Nach Scheidung der ersten Ehe Heirat mit der Grafikerin Johanna Pulfer; 1929 Geburt des Sohnes Rudolf Caspar. Typografische Mitarbeit Johanna Baumbergers bei den meisten späteren Plakaten.

1929
Reise nach Paris, zusammen mit Oscar Lüthy und Walter Kern. Erneuerung der Bekanntschaft etwa mit Ernst Morgentaler und Hans Arp. Im Anschluss daran über längere Zeit Experimente in abstrakter Malerei.

1930
Bezug einer grossen Wohnung mit Atelier im Landsitz «Waid» in Unterengstringen, Zürich.

1932
Auf Betreiben von Otto Rudolf Salvisberg erhält Baumberger einen Lehrauftrag an der Architekturabteilung der ETH für das neue Fach «Beziehung der Farbe zu Bau und Raum». Teilnahme an einer Studienreise in die UdSSR; in den Jahren bis zum Zweiten Weltkrieg zahlreiche weitere Reisen. Dabei entstehen unzählige Skizzen, die Baumberger in seinem Atelier in Aquarelle und Ölbilder überträgt.

1935
Über pädagogische Fragen zunehmend intensivere Auseinandersetzung mit der Anthroposophie, der Baumberger zeitlebens kritisch verbunden bleibt.

1939
Verschiedene reklamegrafische Arbeiten für die Schweizerische Landesausstellung «Landi», darunter das Ausstellungspanorama, sowie Wandmalereien zur Schweizer Geschichte auf dem Höhenweg.

1943
Erster Illustrationszyklus zu Bibelszenen. Auch weitere grafische Arbeiten dieser Art, etwa zu «Faust», «Don Quijotte», «Simplicius Simplicissimus», «Ulenspiegel», «Divina Commedia».

1947
Baumberger wird zum ausserordentlichen Professor an der ETH ernannt.

1949
Ausstellung zum 60. Geburtstag im Kunsthaus Zürich: Gemälde, Aquarelle, Zeichnungen, Lithografien.

1950
Immer freiere Farbgestaltungen, oft zu christologischen Themen, in der Malerei und Grafik der letzten Schaffensjahre. Daneben Publikation vereinzelter Aufsätze und Vorlesungen zu gestaltungs- und kunsttheoretischen Fragen.

1953
Umzug und Rückzug auf den abgelegenen Bruderberg oberhalb von Weiningen, Zürich.

1959
Ausstellung zum 70. Geburtstag in der Graphischen Sammlung der ETH: Auswahl von Arbeiten 1945–1959.

1961
Otto Baumberger stirbt in Weiningen.

Biography of Otto Baumberger

1889
Otto Baumberger born on May 21, 1889, in Altstetten, Zurich. Trains as a lithographer at Emil Winter's Graphic Studio in Zurich after abandoning a textile design apprenticeship. While training he attends the Kunsgewerbeschule and the private Stadler School. His favorite teacher was Eduard Stiefel, who also became famous as a poster designer.

1908
Three years of studies in Munich, Berlin, Paris, and London: Baumberger attends courses at various art schools and academies. Contact with Hermann Huber, Reinhold Kündig, and Hugo Laubi, among others.

1910
Participates in an exhibition for the first time (Zürcher Kunstgesellschaft), where he shows his drawings of the Paris banlieue. Subsequently, and until the 1950s, he is a regular participant in Swiss group exhibitions.

1911
Employed as a lithographer at the J.E. Wolfensberger Graphische Anstalt in Zurich. As a reproductive lithographer, Baumberger gets to know a number of contemporary artists.

1913
Baumberger travels to Paris again and manages to extend his stay by doing poster work for Wolfensberger. Investigates Expressionism and Cubism in painting and graphics. It is only the outbreak of war that compels him to return home and perform military service. Even during the war he remains active, engaged in a broad field of commercial graphic work.

1915
Married Hanni Manz; daughter Gertrud is born in 1918.

1917
The German magazine *Das Plakat* (The poster) surveys Baumberger's work, and includes detailed commentary.

1918
Family difficulties and separation. For a short time serves as the art director for Wolfensberger, "responsible for design and printing," then goes back to working on a freelance basis.

1920
Travels through the poverty-stricken landscape of post-war Germany to Berlin, where he makes contact with publishers and collectors. Engaged as a stage designer at the Deutsches Theater ("Urfaust") upon a recommendation from Max Reinhardt; Baumberger turns down a permanent position.

1922
Back in Zurich, he starts a job as a part-time teacher at the Kunstgewerbeschule. Begins a period of intensive poster production and expands his range of work: commemorative volumes, portfolios of work for the City and Canton of Zurich, stamps for the PTT, book illustrations, murals. Baumberger also works for the *Nebelspalter* (a satirical magazine) and at the Zürich Stadttheater.

1927
After divorcing his first wife, marries the graphic artist Johanna Pulfer; son Rudolf Caspar is born in 1929. Johanna Baumberger does the typographical work for most of her husband's later posters.

1929
Trip to Paris with Oscar Lüthy and Walter Kern. Renews his acquaintances with Ernst Morgenthaler and Hans Arp, among others, which leads to an extended period of experimentation with abstract painting.

1930
Moves into a large apartment with studio at the "Waid" country residence in Unterengstringen, Zurich.

1932
Baumberger is given a contract to lecture in the architecture department of the ETH (Swiss Federal Institute of Technology Zurich) on a new subject– "the relationship of color to structure and space"– on the recommendation of Otto Rudolf Salvisberg. Takes part in a study trip to the USSR and numerous other journeys in the years leading up to World War II. The innumerable sketches from these trips Baumberger reworks as watercolors and oil paintings in his studio.

1935
Pedagogical concerns lead to a more thorough study of anthroposophy, with which Baumberger remains critically associated throughout his life.

1939
Various graphic design work for the "Landi" Swiss Federal Exhibition, including the exhibition panorama and murals of Swiss history on the "Höhenweg."

1943
First cycle of illustrations of Biblical scenes. Does further graphic work of this kind, such as for *Faust, Don Quixote, Simplicius Simplicissimus, Ulenspiegel,* and the *Divine Comedy.*

1947
Baumberger appointed associate professor at the ETH.

1949
Exhibition for his sixtieth birthday at the Kunsthaus in Zurich: paintings, watercolors, drawings, lithographs.

1950
Increasingly abstract color designs, often on Christological subjects, in the painting and graphic work of his last creative years. Also publishes occasional essays and lectures on design and art theory topics.

1953
Moves to retreat in the remote Bruderberg, above Weiningen, Zurich.

1959
Exhibition for his seventieth birthday at the ETH Graphische Sammlung: selected works, 1945–59.

1961
Otto Baumberger dies in Weiningen.

Katalog

Alle abgebildeten Plakate sowie der Plakatentwurf von Otto Baumberger stammen aus der Plakatsammlung des Museum für Gestaltung Zürich. Die Plakate sind in der Schweiz erschienen.

Die Daten des Katalogs folgen den Rubriken Plakattext, Erscheinungsjahr, Druck- bzw. Entwurfstechnik, Format. Dabei gelten folgende Regelungen:

Plakattext: Die beste Textwiedergabe bildet die Abbildung des Plakates selbst. Darum wird hier eine vereinfachte Form wiedergegeben, welche nur die aussagekräftigen Textbestandteile berücksichtigt. Allfällige Umstellungen dienen der Verständlichkeit. Das Zeichen / trennt inhaltliche Texteinheiten.

Format: Die Angaben werden in der Abfolge Höhe x Breite und in cm gemacht. Weil die Plakate oft nicht exakt rechtwinklig geschnitten sind, werden die Abmessungen auf halbe cm aufgerundet.

Die Plakatgeschichte ist ein junges Forschungsgebiet – verlässliche Hinweise sind rar. Jeder Hinweis und jede Ergänzung sind willkommen: plakatsammlung@museum-gestaltung.ch

Catalogue

All posters reproduced are from the Museum für Gestaltung Zürich's Poster Collection. All the posters were published in Switzerland.

The data listed in the catalog is broken down into the following sections: poster title and/or text, year of first appearance, printing or design technique, and size. In particular, the following rules have been applied:

Poster text: The poster itself provides the best version of the text, and thus a simplified form is used which provides only the most meaningful elements. Any rearrangements that have been made are for purposes of intelligibility. A slash mark separates textual units by content.

Format: The dimensions are given in centimeters as height x width. Because posters are often not cut exactly at right angles, the dimensions are rounded off to the half-centimeter.

The history of posters is a recent field of research – reliable information is rare. Any further references or additional material are welcome: plakatsammlung@museum-gestaltung.ch

1 Wer rechnet kauft im Globus
Anyone who counts buys at Globus
1934
Gouache, Tempera (Plakatentwurf) – Gouache, tempera (poster design)
126,5 × 89 cm

2 Seiden-Grieder Zürich
1913
Lithografie – Lithograph
127 × 90 cm

3 Senft / Basel
1916
Lithografie – Lithograph
127 × 90 cm

4 Martini / Der Steiger
The climber
1927
Lithografie – Lithograph
128 × 90,5 cm

5 Balatum / Spottbilliger und dauerhafter Bodenbelag
Dirt cheap and durable floor covering
1928
Lithografie – Lithograph
128 × 90,5 cm

6 Chiropraktik Nein
No to chiropractics
1938
Lithografie – Lithograph
127 × 90 cm

7 Baumann / Bahnhofstr. 25
1919
Lithografie – Lithograph
127 × 90 cm

8 Remington / A. Waltisbühl & Co Zürich
ca. 1918
Lithografie – Lithograph
127 × 90 cm

9 Büro Einrichtungen Anton Waltisbühl / Remington-Haus Zürich
Office furnishings
1912
Lithografie – Lithograph
106 × 76 cm

10 Bodenwichse Parkettglanz / Garant. Schweizerfabrikat
Parkettglanz floor wax / Guaranteed Swiss product
ca. 1921
Lithografie – Lithograph
127 × 90 cm

11 Gygax & Limberger / Möbelfabrik Zürich
Zurich furniture factory
1911
Lithografie – Lithograph
127 × 90 cm

12 Kunsthaus-Maskenball / Baur au Lac
Kunsthaus Masked ball
1932
Lithografie – Lithograph
127 × 90 cm

13 Waterman / Die Füllfeder
The fountain pen
1915
Lithografie – Lithograph
127 × 90 cm

14 Durol / Allerfeinstes Automotoren-Oel / H. R. Koller & Co. Winterthur
Durol / The very finest motor oil
ca. 1923
Lithografie – Lithograph
127 × 90 cm

15 Hürlimann-Bier / Kriegszeit / Friedenszeit
Hürlimann-Beer / Wartime / Peacetime
ca. 1920
Lithografie – Lithograph
64 × 90 cm

16 Speck's Cinema / Haus du Pont
1913
Lithografie – Lithograph
127 x 90 cm

17 Kunsthaus / Maskenfest / Baur au Lac Zürich
Kunsthaus / Masquerade party
1926
Lithografie – Lithograph
127 × 90 cm

18 Trinkt Zürcher Löwenbräu!
Drink Zurich Löwenbräu!
1927
Lithografie – Lithograph
127 × 90 cm

19 Walsheim Neger / Walsheim Brauerei A.G. / Walsheim dark beer
1929
Lithografie – Lithograph
110 × 70,5 cm

20 Diese Politik der grossen Worte hat nichts erreicht! Freisinnige Politik der Tat hat die städtischen Finanzen geordnet und die Steuerlast vermindert! Stimmt Freisinnig Liste 6
This policy of big talk has achieved nothing! Liberal action policy has put the municipal finances in order and reduced the tax burden! Vote Freisinnig List 6
ca. 1925
Lithografie – Lithograph
127 × 90 cm

21 Wählt Sozialdemokraten
Vote Social Democrats
ca. 1925
Lithografie – Lithograph
126 × 90 cm

22 Marke «Tell» Schuhe / Schuhfabrik Frauenfeld
"Tell" brand shoes / Frauenfeld shoe factory
1924
Lithografie – Lithograph
128 × 90,5 cm

23 Die weisse Mode / Doelker
The white fashion / Doelker
1923
Lithografie – Lithograph
127 × 90 cm

24 Kauft den Qualitätsschuh Bally «Farmer» – Buy the Bally "Farmer" quality shoe
1924
Lithografie – Lithograph
127 × 90 cm

25 Grosser Schuhmarkt / Dosenbach – Mega shoe store
ca. 1920
Lithografie – Lithograph
127 × 90 cm

26 Bally / Schuhe für gute Arbeit
Bally / Shoes for good work
1934
Lithografie – Lithograph
127 × 90 cm

27 Kauft Qualitätsschuhe in der Goldkugel AG Schaffhausen
Buy quality shoes at Goldkugel AG Schaffhausen
1920
Lithografie – Lithograph
127 × 90 cm

28 Wollt Ihr solche Frauen?
Frauenstimmrecht Nein
Do you want women like this?
No to women's suffrage
1920
Lithografie – Lithograph
127 × 90 cm

29 Marque PKZ
1923
Lithografie – Lithograph
128 × 90,5 cm

30 14 Tage Preissturz im PKZ
14 days of falling prices at the PKZ
1923
Lithografie – Lithograph
127 × 90 cm

31 PKZ zieht um
PKZ is moving
1925
Lithografie – Lithograph
128 × 90 cm

32 PKZ hat Teilausverkauf
Sales at PKZ
1922
Lithografie – Lithograph
127 × 90 cm

33 PKZ / Knips-Konkurrenz
PKZ / Snapshot competition
1923
Lithografie – Lithograph
127 × 90 cm

34 PKZ / Regentrotz /
Der garantiert wasserdichte
PKZ Regenmantel
PKZ / Rain-resister / The guaranteed
waterproof PKZ raincoat
1924
Lithografie – Lithograph
127 × 90 cm

35 Forster / Teil-Ausverkauf
Sales
1930
Lithografie – Lithograph
127 × 90 cm

36 Ausverkauf Forster & Co. /
Teppichhaus Zürich
Forster & Co. sales /
Zurich carpet store
1926
Lithografie – Lithograph
128 × 90,5 cm

37 Art. Inst. Orell Füssli Zürich
1928
Lithografie – Lithograph
127 × 90 cm

38 Möbel-Hurst Zürich
Hurst Furniture, Zurich
ca. 1924
Lithografie – Lithograph
127 × 90 cm

39 Dosenbach's grosser
Schuhmarkt
Dosenbach's mega shoe store
1915
Lithografie – Lithograph
127 × 90 cm

40 Forster / Teilausverkauf
Forster / Sales
1928
Lithografie – Lithograph
127 × 90 cm

41 Fretz Fahrplan / Zuverlässig
und praktisch
Fretz timetable / Reliable and
practical
1923
Lithografie – Lithograph
127 × 90 cm

42 Wir ziehen ins Metropol!
Geschw. Severin, Zürich
We are moving to the Metropol!
Severin Siblings, Zurich
1911
Lithografie – Lithograph
37,5 × 98 cm

43 Corso / Täglich nachmittags
& abends Künstlerkonzerte /
Restaurants / soignierte Küche
und Keller – Corso / Artiste concerts every afternoon & evening /
Restaurants / refined cuisine
and wine cellar
1911
Lithografie – Lithograph
124 × 94 cm

44 Küchen-Erpf / Erstes Zürcher
Küchenausstattungsgeschäft
A, Erpf & Co – Erpf Kitchens /
Zurich's first kitchen appliance
shop A. Erpf & Co
1913
Lithografie – Lithograph
127 × 90 cm

45 Restaurant du Pont. Zürich
1913
Lithografie – Lithograph
127 × 90 cm

46 Schweizer / helft euern
heimgekehrten Brüdern /
Rückwandererhilfe – Swiss
citizens / help your returning
brothers / Help with repatriation
1943
Lithografie – Lithograph
127 × 90 cm

47 Stadt-Polizei / Telefon 17
Municipal police / Telephone 17
1931
Lithografie – Lithograph
127 × 90 cm

48 Städtisches Fundbüro
Municipal lost property office
1931
Lithografie – Lithograph
90 × 64 cm

49 Jecklin
1918
Lithografie – Lithograph
127 × 90 cm

50 Turmac Reginaris
1933
Lithografie – Lithograph
127 × 90 cm

51 Rennwegtor Kleiderstoffe /
Ca. Zellweger & Co., Zürich
Rennwegtor dress fabric /
Ca. Zellweger & Co., Zurich
1931
Lithografie – Lithograph
127 × 90 cm

52 Fein-Kaller
1930
Lithografie – Lithograph
128 × 90,5 cm

53 Swan
1919
Lithografie – Lithograph
127 × 90 cm

54 Brak Bitter
1937
Lithografie – Lithograph
128 × 90,5 cm

55 R. Gasteyger & Co.
Zürich / Herren und Knaben
Bekleidung – Men's and
boys' clothing
1911
Lithografie – Lithograph
106 × 76 cm

56 Konzerte / Wiener Männergesangsverein – Concerts / Vienna
Men's Choir
1917
Lithografie – Lithograph
127 × 90 cm

57 Hotel St. Gotthard Zürich
1917
Lithografie – Lithograph
128 × 90,5 cm

58 Kunstgewerbemuseum der Stadt Zürich / Ausstellung Beleuchtungskörper
Lighting fixtures exhibit
1917
Lithografie – Lithograph
123 × 83 cm

59 Gastspiel Professor Arthur Nikisch
Guest performance by Professor Arthur Nikisch
1917
Lithografie – Lithograph
127 × 90 cm

60 Wiener Café Splendid Zürich / Künstler Conzerte
Artiste concerts
1915
Lithografie – Lithograph
127 × 90 cm

61 Sträuli Seifen Winterthur
Sträuli soaps Wintherthur
1925
Lithografie – Lithograph
128 × 90,5 cm

62 Medea
1917
Lithografie – Lithograph
127 × 89 cm

63 Sammelt Steinfels-Bilder
Collect Steinfels pictures
1934
Lithografie – Lithograph
127 × 90 cm

64 Lichtspiele Speck's Palast / Erstaufführung / Untersee Expedition – Speck's Palast cinema / Première / Underwater Expedition
1916
Lithografie – Lithograph
126 × 89 cm

65 Motor Comptoir Zürich
1932
Lithografie – Lithograph
127 × 90 cm

66 IV. Internationales Flugmeeting Zürich – 4th Zurich International Air Show
1937
Lithografie – Lithograph
127 × 90 cm

67 Hier telephonieren!
Telephone here!
1933
Lithografie – Lithograph
127 × 90 cm

68 *Neue Zürcher Zeitung* / Erscheint dreimal täglich / Führendes Blatt der Schweiz in Politik Handel Wissenschaft und Kunst
Neue Zürcher Zeitung / Appears three times daily / Switzerland's leading newspaper for politics, science, and art
1928
Lithografie – Lithograph
128 × 90,5 cm

69 Zoologischer Garten Zürich
Zurich Zoological Gardens
1929
Lithografie – Lithograph
127 × 90 cm

70 Zwicky Näh- & Stickseide
Zwicky sewing and embroidery silk
1927
Lithografie – Lithograph
127 × 90 cm

71 Interniert / Das Internationale Komitee vom Roten Kreuz hilft!
Interned / The International Red Cross Committee helps!
1943
Lithografie – Lithograph
128 × 90 cm

72 Muttertag – Mother's Day
1932
Lithografie – Lithograph
127 × 90 cm

73 Kriegsopfer / Das Internationale Komitee vom Roten Kreuz hilft!
War victims / The International Red Cross Committee helps!
1943
Lithografie – Lithograph
127 × 90 cm

74 Pro Juventute / Marken und Kartenverkauf zu Gunsten der Schulentlassenen
Pro Juventute / Stamp and ticket sales to benefit graduates
1930
Lithografie – Lithograph
127 × 90 cm

75 Zürich rot! Wählt sozialdemokratisch / Liste 4
Red Zurich! Vote Social Democrat / List 4
1931
Lithografie – Lithograph
127 × 90 cm

76 Beachtet die Schaufenster mit dem Plakat der Schweizerwoche
Watch for the shop windows with the "Swiss Week" poster
1919
Lithografie – Lithograph
127 × 90 cm

77 Turnus / Ausstellung des Schweiz. Kunstverein
Exhibition by the Swiss Art Association
1919
Lithografie – Lithograph
100 × 70 cm

78 650 Jahre Eidgenossenschaft / Bundesfeier-Spiel Schwyz
650 years of the Confederation / Schwyz Federal Celebration Games
1941
Lithografie – Lithograph
128 × 91 cm

79 Hütet euch vor dem Versailler Völkerbund
Beware of the Versailles League of Nations
1920
Lithografie – Lithograph
127 × 90 cm

80 Sammelt Steinfels-Bilder
Collect Steinfels pictures
1934
Lithografie – Lithograph
127 × 90 cm

81 Ur-Hell / Wädenswiler Spezial-Bier – Premium light / Wädenswiler special beer
ca. 1925
Lithografie – Lithograph
127 × 90 cm

82 Internationales Flugmeeting Zürich – Zurich International Air Show
1932 Lithografie – Lithograph
127 × 90 cm

83 Gang, lueg d'Heimet a! 650 Jahre Eidgenossenschaft 1291–1941
Go visit your homeland! 650 years of Confederation 1291–1941
1941
Lithografie – Lithograph
127 × 90 cm

84 Thermalkurort Baden Schweiz
Thermal spa, Baden, Switzerland
1916
Lithografie – Lithograph
127 × 89 cm

85 Jungfraubahn Schweiz
Jungfrau railway, Switzerland
1924
Lithografie – Lithograph
127 × 90 cm

86 Einsiedeln
1934
Lithografie – Lithograph
100 × 70 cm

87 Schöllenen-Bahn
Schöllenen railway
1919
Lithografie – Lithograph
128 × 90,5 cm

88 Gstaad / Das elegante
Schwimmbad im Berner Oberland
The elegant swimming pool
in the Bernese Oberland
1929
Lithografie – Lithograph
127 × 90 cm

89 Enzian Bergriese
1923
Lithografie – Lithograph
127 × 90 cm

90 Vierwaldstättersee
Lake Lucerne
1928
Lithografie – Lithograph
127 × 90 cm

91 Davos / Schweiz / Switzerland /
Suisse
1932
Lithografie – Lithograph
102 × 64 cm

92 Höll-Grotten / Baar bei Zug /
Wundervolle Tropfsteinhöhlen
Höll Grottoes / Baar near Zug /
Wonderful caves with stalactites
and stalagmites
ca. 1931
Lithografie – Lithograph
127 × 90 cm

93 Zurich / Switzerland's
metropolis – Zürich /
Die Metropole der Schweiz
1929
Lithografie – Lithograph
100 × 64 cm

94 Zurich
1916
Lithografie – Lithograph
127 × 90 cm

95 Vierwaldstättersee
Lake Lucerne
1928
Lithografie – Lithograph
127 × 89 cm

96 Glarnerland / Walensee
1944
Lithografie – Lithograph
101 × 63 cm

97 Zürichsee – Lake Zurich
1935
Lithografie – Lithograph
100 × 70 cm

Bibliografie / Bibliography

Otto Baumberger findet als Maler, Zeichner und Grafiker in vielen Publikationen und Ausstellungskatalogen Erwähnung und ist darin mit Abbildungen seiner Arbeiten vertreten. Zudem hat er zahlreiche literarische Werke illustriert. In der vorliegenden Liste ausgewählter Publikationen sind jedoch nur Titel angeführt, die Baumberger als Plakatgestalter würdigen oder ihn innerhalb der Schweizer Plakatgeschichte positionieren. Zusätzlich wurden eigene Schriften Baumbergers berücksichtigt, so Zeitungsartikel zu grafischen Themen und autobiografische Aufzeichnungen Baumbergers.

Otto Baumberger appears as a painter, draftsman, and graphic artist in the publications and exhibition catalogues in which his work has been reproduced. He also illustrated numerous literary works. However, this list of selected publications features only those titles that acknowledge Baumberger as a poster designer, or situate him within Swiss poster history. Some writings by Baumberger have also been included, such as newspaper articles dealing with graphics, and autobiographical notes.

Baumberger, Otto, «Wahrheit in der Reklame (Entgegnung eines Graphikers)», in: *Neue Zürcher Zeitung*, 24. 5. 1933.

Baumberger, Otto, «Aus der Lehrzeit eines Graphikers», in: *Neue Zürcher Zeitung*, 20. 8. 1933.

Baumberger, Otto, «J.E. Wolfensberger zum 70. Geburtstag am 18. Juni», in: *Neue Zürcher Zeitung*, 18. 6. 1943.

Baumberger, Otto, *Der innere Weg eines Malers. Aus persönlichen Aufzeichnungen*, Zürich / Stuttgart 1963.

Baumberger, Otto, *Blick nach aussen und innen – Autobiografische Aufzeichnungen*, Weiningen-Zürich 1966.

Bernoulli, Rudolf, «Neue Schweizer Plakate», in: *Das Plakat*, 11, 1920, S. 495–504.

Bibliothèque Forney Paris, *Objets – Réalismes: Affiches Suisses 1905–1950*, Ausstellungskatalog, Paris 1982.

Evers, Bernd (Ed.), *Schweizerware, Ein Jahrhundert im Weltformat, Schweizer Plakate von 1900 bis zur Gegenwart*, Staatliche Museen zu Berlin, Berlin 2001.

Gewerbemuseum Basel, *Das Schweizer Plakat 1900–1984*, Basel 1984.

Giroud, Jean-Charles, Michel Schlup (Ed.), *Les artistes suisses et l'affiche, Un siècle de fascination et de confrontation*, Neuchâtel 2001.

Giroud, Jean-Charles, *Les images d'un rêve, Deux siècles d'affiches patriotiques suisses*, Genf 2005.

Giroud, Jean-Charles, Michel Schlup (Ed.), *Paradis à vendre, Un siècle d'affiches touristiques suisses*, Genf 2005.

Giroud, Jean-Charles, *L'Art Nouveau et l'affiche suisse*, Genf 2006.

Kellenberger, Erich, «Die Werbung der Wirklichkeit», in: *Weltwoche-Magazin*, 10.3.1982.

Kern, Walter, «Das Plakat», in: *Das Werk*, Heft 8, August 1943, S. 237–241.

Kern, Walter, «Otto Baumberger, Kunsthaus Zürich, 14. Januar bis 12. Februar 1950», in: *Das Werk*, Heft 3, März 1950, S. 27.

Kunstgewerbemuseum Zürich, *Meister der Plakatkunst*, Ausstellungskatalog (Wegleitung 229), Zürich 1959.

Kunstgewerbemuseum Zürich, *Kulturelle Plakate der Schweiz*, Ausstellungskatalog (Wegleitung 293), Zürich 1974.

Kunstgewerbemuseum Zürich, *Werbestil 1930–1940. Die alltägliche Bildersprache eines Jahrzehnts*, Ausstellungskatalog (Wegleitung 335), Zürich 1981.

Kunstgewerbemuseum Zürich, *Ferdinand Hodler und das Schweizer Künstlerplakat*, Ausstellungskatalog (Wegleitung 346), Zürich 1983.

Margadant, Bruno, *Das Schweizer Plakat 1900–1983*, Basel 1983.

Museum für Gestaltung Zürich, *Otto Baumberger 1889–1961*, (Reihe Schweizer Plakatgestalter 4), hrsg. von Martin Heller, Ausstellungskatalog (Wegleitung 365), Zürich 1988.

Roethlisberger, Hermann, «Vom Schweizerischen Plakat», in: *O mein Heimatland*, 1917, S. 81–120.

Rotzler, Willy, *Otto Baumberger. Ein Pionier der Schweizer Plakatkunst*, Bern 1983.

Sachs, Hans, «Otto Baumberger», in: *Das Plakat*, Juli 1917, S. 185–194.

Wobmann, Karl, Willy Rotzler, *Touristikplakate der Schweiz 1880–1940*, Aarau 1980.

Wobmann, Karl, Willy Rotzler, *Politische und soziale Plakate der Schweiz*, Zürich 1985.

Martin Heller
Martin Heller, geboren 1952. Künstlerische Ausbildung sowie Studium der Kunstgeschichte, Ethnologie und Volkskunde in Basel. Ab 1986 Kurator, dann ab 1990 Direktor des Museum für Gestaltung Zürich. Zahlreiche Ausstellungen und Publikationen, insbesondere zu Design, Fotografie, Kunst, Medien, Populärkultur. Lehrveranstaltungen und Vorträge im In- und Ausland. Von 1999 bis 2003 Künstlerischer Direktor der Schweizer Landesausstellung Expo.02. 2003 Gründung von Heller Enterprises, Zürich. Kulturprojekte in Deutschland, Österreich und der Schweiz, darunter die Intendanz für Linz 2009 Kulturhauptstadt Europas.

Born in 1952. Trained as an artist and studied art history and social anthropology in Basel. From 1986 served as curator, and from 1990 as director of the Museum für Gestaltung Zürich. Organized numerous exhibitions and publications, with a particular focus on design, photography, art, media, and popular culture. Has taught and lectured both in Switzerland and abroad. From 1999 to 2003 served as artistic director of the Swiss National Exhibition Expo.02. In 2003 founded Heller Enterprises, Zurich, which organizes cultural projects in Germany, Austria, and Switzerland, including the artistic direction of Linz as the cultural capital of Europe in 2009.

Bettina Richter
Geboren 1964 in Basel. Studium der Kunstgeschichte, Germanistik und Romanistik in Heidelberg, Paris und Zürich. 1996 Dissertation über die Antikriegsgrafiken von Théophile-Alexandre Steinlen. 1997–2006 wissenschaftliche Mitarbeiterin in der Plakatsammlung des Museum für Gestaltung Zürich. Seit 2006 Kuratorin der Plakatsammlung. Nebenbei Tätigkeit als Dozentin an der Zürcher Hochschule der Künste sowie als freischaffende Autorin.

Born 1964 in Basel. Studied art history, German, and Romance languages in Heidelberg, Paris, and Zurich. 1996 dissertation on the antiwar graphics of Théophile-Alexandre Steinlen. From 1997 to 2006 served as a research associate in the Poster Collection of the Museum für Gestaltung Zürich, and as Curator of the same since 2006. Also lectures at the Zürcher Hochschule der Künste and works as a freelance writer.

Eine Publikation des Museum für Gestaltung Zürich
Christian Brändle, Direktor

A Publication of the Museum für Gestaltung Zürich
Christian Brändle, Director

Otto Baumberger
Konzept, Redaktion / Concept and editing:
Bettina Richter, Christina Reble, Balthasar Zimmermann
Gestaltung / Design: Integral Lars Müller
Übersetzung / Translation: Michael Robinson
Lektorat Deutsch / German Copyediting: Angela Kuhk
Lektorat Englisch / English Copyediting: Jonathan Fox
Lithografie / Repro: Lithotronic
Druck / Printing: Konkordia GmbH
Einband / Binding: Josef Spinner Großbuchbinderei GmbH

Reihe / «Poster Collection» Series
Herausgegeben von / Edited by
Museum für Gestaltung Zürich, Plakatsammlung
Bettina Richter, Kuratorin der Plakatsammlung / Curator of the Poster Collection
Verena Formanek, Leiterin Sammlungen / Head of Collections
In Zusammenarbeit mit / In cooperation with
Christina Reble, Publikationen / Publications Museum für Gestaltung Zürich

Museum für Gestaltung Zürich
Ausstellungsstrasse 60
CH-8005 Zürich / Switzerland
www.museum-gestaltung.ch

Museum für Gestaltung Zürich
Plakatsammlung / Poster Collection
CH-8005 Zürich / Switzerland
plakatsammlung@museum-gestaltung.ch

Lars Müller Publishers
CH-5400 Baden / Switzerland
books@lars-muller.ch
www.lars-muller-publishers.com

ISBN: 978-3-03778-129-6
Erste Auflage / First Edition 2008

Printed in Germany

Wir danken für Unterstützung
For their support we wish to thank

apg Affichage